THE BIBLICAL MANDATE FOR CARING FOR CREATION

THE BIBLICAL MANDATE FOR

Caring for Creation

DICK TRIPP

Exploring Faith Today
Title No. 23

WIPF & STOCK · Eugene, Oregon

*To my wife Sally, whose love of nature
and concern for the environment has
been a growing inspiration over the years*

THE BIBLICAL MANDATE FOR CARING FOR CREATION

Except where otherwise noted, all scripture quotations are taken from the Holy Bible, Today's New International Version® TNIV® Copyright © 2001, 2005 by Biblica, Inc™.

Thanks to Christian Education Publications for permission to reproduce the prayer on page 64 from David Jenkins' book *Further Everyday Prayers.*

Wipf & Stock
A Division of Wipf and Stock Publishers
199 W. 8th Ave., Suite 3
Eugene, OR 97401

www.wipfandstock.com

ISBN 13: 978-1-62032-722-7

Contents

Foreword

In a beautiful and breathtaking vision, the person who was inspired to write Psalm 104 was given a panoramic view of God's creative power in and through the awesomeness and diversity of life on earth, and of the creation of the earth itself.

The picture here is that everything originally derives from the wisdom and light of God: the skies, the planet, vegetation, animals and people. God made them all and they witness to God's wisdom in their making. Even though the neighbouring people of Canaan thought that the sea was a demigod of chaotic power, this Psalm shows the creator God ordering the chaos of the waters into life-giving springs and rivers. God provides food as well as the animating breath of life itself. The words 'breath' and 'spirit' are the same in Hebrew, meaning the breath of living creatures is the same as the breath of God. This breath is still the giver of life to these creatures. God's breath brings new creatures into being and God's 'face' is made to 'renew the face of the ground.' Plants, yielding wine, are a means of pleasure; sustenance and oil are means of God-given hospitality and joy. Even trees, which provide hospitality for birds and animals, witness to the bounty, abundance and providence of God in all that God has made and given. Although, as Genesis describes it, the earth has experienced fallenness, nevertheless, the original intention and power of God are yet visible in what God has made.

A key principle of the psalm, especially in verse 35, is that no-one should harm or interfere with the operation of the world as God intends it. We are called to give, in thanksgiving and responsible stewardship, the whole of ourselves to God in life so that we may care for the world we have been given. When a creature is not able to live out, or to realize, its God-given potential, then that creature is not able to witness fully to the glory of God. For this reason, a challenge to or the destruction of God's design can threaten the delicate balance God has put in place and our own destiny. In Psalm 104, we are totally bound up with the existence and destiny of everything else; with springs and hills and trees and creeping things. We are called in Genesis 2:15 to serve and keep the Garden of Eden rather than to consume and dominate it. Our dominion in creation is a dominion of upholding, sustaining and redeeming care.

This vision is centred in Christ in a remarkable way in the New Testament, in Paul's letter to the Colossians 1:15–20. Here Christ is God's image, God's wisdom, the first-born of all creation, the second person of the Holy Trinity, the creative Word, the principle in which all things are created and in which everything holds together.

For followers of Christ then, there is a special responsibility to become deeply involved in creation and the redemption of all things by beginning with people; with the salvation of the soul. From this flows the salvation of the whole earth as people with soul love and keep what God has given in all of life. Jesus said God's Kingdom would come on this earth (and not another) as it is in heaven.

Dick Tripp, in this comprehensive expression of the biblical mandate for caring for God's creation, has provided Christians with a detailed biblical approach to the growing crisis in our environment, to its causes, the role of the Christian Church, and the challenge that lies before us all. What is needed today is the energy and morale for people at the flax roots to act decisively and together. Dick's work provides the biblical and spiritual motivation we need to move forward at this critical time. The moral leadership the church can offer is very significant, not only because, as the environmental groups say, our very planet is at stake, but also because it is God's earth, our home. We are accountable to the creator of the heavens and the earth for our stewardship in this garden for which we have been called to care.

I am sure that readers of this well-researched and intelligently argued resource will be given an irresistible biblical vision and mandate to redeem what is being despoiled.

++David Moxon
Archbishop of the New Zealand Dioceses
Primate of the Anglican Church in
Aotearoa New Zealand and Polynesia

Acknowledgements

I wish to thank the many folk who have given encouragement and advice in writing all the titles in this series. Particularly I thank my wife Sally for her computer skills and her patience; my son Tim for his creative cover designs and managing the website; Merritt Smith for his thorough proofreading of this book; and David Moxon for writing the foreword. Above all, I wish to thank all who pray for this ministry.

Introduction

This book has one main purpose: to explore in a logical manner all that the Bible has to say about our human responsibility to care for God's creation, from Genesis to Revelation. Over the past decade or two there have been some excellent books written on the subject. I have listed those I have read and found helpful, at the end of this book. I have sought to take those points I consider most significant from each and put them in a logical order, allowing the Bible to provide the framework and speak for itself as much as possible. Where I have used several quotes from the one author, I have put the title of the book only in the first instance. The survival and wellbeing of the human race provides a most compelling reason for facing this issue today. However, regardless of this, it is the revelation of scripture, what God himself thinks about his creation, that should provide the most compelling reason of all for Christians to be concerned about it.

Before launching into this main theme of what the Bible has to say on the subject, I have thought it would be helpful to give five introductory chapters summarising the growing crisis: causes that have led us into it, the modern environmental movement and the positive and negative influences of Christianity. Although of necessity sketchy, these will provide a background before starting on the biblical material. Some of the books listed at the end deal more fully with these issues for those who want more.

It took a number of years for the early Christians' vision to be enlarged enough to include the Gentiles fully. It took about 400 years for the church to sort out what the New Testament was saying about the trinitarian nature of God. It took a further 1100 years to spell out clearly justification by faith alone. It took another 400 years to come to terms with the priesthood of the laity, and the gifts and ministry of the Spirit. Over the last 50 years the church has begun to take more seriously what the Bible tells us about creation. Though it has been forced upon us by the events of the last few decades, let us make sure we listen carefully to all that God is saying. As Aquinas put it succinctly, 'Any error about creation also leads to an error about God.'

Ian Bradley said well, 20 years ago, in *God is Green: Ecology for Christians*:

> What we need is not, as is so often argued … a new theology of nature but rather a return to the original message contained in the Bible and preached and practised by the early Church …
>
> Greening Christianity does not involve grafting it on some alien philosophy but simply restoring its original character. Indeed, it means stripping off a whole series of alien layers that have accumulated to reveal the original greenness of the Garden of Eden and the cross on Calvary.

CHAPTER 1

The growing crisis

Contemporary environmental activist and writer David Orr, in *Ecological Literacy: Education and the Transition to a Postmodern World*, says:

> The crisis of sustainability, the fit between humanity and its habitat, is manifest in varying ways and degrees everywhere on earth. It is not only a permanent feature of the public agenda; for all practical purposes it is the agenda. No other issue of politics, economics, and public policy will remain unaffected by the crisis of resources, population, climate change, species extinction, acid rain, deforestation, ozone depletion, and soil loss. Sustainability is about the terms and conditions of human survival, and yet we still educate at all levels as if no such crisis exists.

We humans have not made a very good job of caring for planet earth, particularly over the past century. The following selected details, taken from a variety of sources, seem to me to be particularly significant. Scores more worldwide could be cited but these will highlight the problem.

Climate change

NASA scientist James Hansen, widely regarded as the world's leading climate scientist, says that 350 parts per million of carbon dioxide in the atmosphere is the limit if we want to avoid major catastrophe. At the time of writing it is in the 390s and rising.

A report from the World Humanitarian Forum, led by Kofi Annan, the former UN Secretary-General, suggests that global warming is already killing an estimated 300,000 people a year. Ninety percent of those deaths

are related to environmental degradation resulting from climate change —
principally malnutrition, diarrhoea and malaria. The remaining ten
percent are linked to weather-related disasters. This figure is projected to
rise to 500,000 by 2030. According to the United Nations, climate change
will result in at least an additional 150 million environmental refugees by
2050.

Michael Northcott, in *A Moral Climate,* says that in the last 300 years
600,000 million tonnes of the carbon formerly locked in the earth has
been dug up and added to the carbon cycle.

According to the Carbon Dioxide Information Analysis Center, in the
past 400,000 years the planet has never had so much carbon dioxide in its
atmosphere as it does today, and the levels are continuing to rise.

1998 set a record for economic losses from weather-related disasters
up to that time, with an estimated $90 billion worth of damage, not to
mention that 32,000 people died and another 300 million people were
displaced. Hurricane Mitch in Central America, the flooding of China's
Yangtze River, floods in Turkey, Argentina and Bangladesh, fires in Siberia,
an ice storm in New England — the list is staggering. Hurricane Katrina
was only the fourth recorded Category Five hurricane to have made
landfall in the United States and the seventh Category Five hurricane
to have maintained that status longer than 30 hours. It was followed
by another Category Five hurricane, Rita, the fourth most powerful on
record, and soon after by Wilma, the strongest Atlantic hurricane ever
recorded.

It has been estimated that the cost of climate-related disasters for the
next 20 years will be us$6–10 trillion, ten times current aid levels.

The end-of-summer Arctic sea ice area was 40 percent less in
2007 than in the late 1970s when accurate satellite measurements
began. Climate models had not predicted such a large loss before the
middle of the twenty-first century. James Hansen says in *Storms of My
Grandchildren,* 'I have found no Arctic researcher who believes that sea
ice will survive if the world continues with business-as-usual fossil fuel
use.' The Greenland and West Antarctic ice sheets are each losing mass
at more than 100 cubic kilometres per year, and the sea level is rising at
more than three centimetres per decade. Glacial shrinkage worldwide is
causing flooding and lack of water in many places.

According to Northcott, human-induced global warming threatens the collapse of whole ecosystems, from the poles to the heart of Africa, and the extinction of up to 40 percent of the earth's species.

Professor Sir Ghillean Prance is an expert in biodiversity and plant taxonomy. Formerly director of the Royal Botanical Gardens at Key, he is currently director of the Eden Project. He is responsible for introducing 450 Amazonian plant species to science. He thinks so-called climate sceptics are like ostriches burying their heads in the sand.

Ozone loss

The British Antarctic Survey station at Halley Bay detected slight ozone declines in the 1970s, greater declines in the 1980s, 30 percent depletion by 1984 and up to 70 percent depletion in the spring in recent decades.

Waste

According to the Rev Dr Rob Frost, in the foreword of *Planetwise* by Dave Bookless, the world produces 2 million tonnes of rubbish every day. Half a billion tonnes of oil are spilled every year through accidents, dumping and leakage. Six and a half million tonnes of refuse, including toxic and non-biodegradable waste, is discharged every year into the world's oceans.

According to William McDonough and Michael Braungart in *Cradle to Cradle: Remaking the Way We Make Things,* apart from waste that occurs from use, 90 percent of the materials used in the process of making are wasted even before the end product appears in a store. Waste products of industrialism are now evident on every continent, and in every patch of ocean.

According to the U.S. Environmental Protection Agency and U.S. Bureau of Mines, in the U.S. only 1.5 percent of waste is municipal garbage. Seventy-five percent comes from mining, oil and gas production, 13 percent from agriculture, 9.5 percent from industry, and one percent from sewage.

Steven Bouma-Prediger, in *For the Beauty of the Earth,* says that in the U.S. enough aluminium is thrown away to rebuild the country's entire commercial airline fleet every three months. Enough disposable nappies are discarded each year to reach to the moon and back seven times, if linked end-to-end.

All this is contrary to the way God has structured nature. John Muir, in *My First Summer in the Sierra*, said:

> One is constantly reminded of the infinite lavishness and fertility of Nature — inexhaustible abundance amid what seems enormous waste. And yet when we look into any of her operations that lie within the reach of our minds, we learn that no particle of her material is wasted or worn out. It is eternally flowing from use to use, beauty to yet higher beauty.

Dave Bookless says, 'God made a world where nothing is wasted and it dishonours him if I am careless with what he has made.' Studies show that three out of five African Americans in the U.S. live near abandoned toxic waste sites. The illegal 'exports' and 'imports' of used plastics and other waste material are causing harm to many of the poor in India, Indonesia, the Philippines and other developing nations. This is what Sallie McFague describes as 'environmental racism'.

Water

There is a plastic soup in the Pacific twice the size of the U.S. It stretches from 500 miles off the Californian coast all the way to Japan. In a 1999 study, the North Pacific was found to contain six pounds of plastic for each pound of surface zooplankton. Though plastic continues to break down into smaller and smaller pieces, they are still composed of plastic polymers. Harm to fish and birds that ingest it is incalculable. We are stuck with it forever. The phytoplankton in the seas, together with the rainforests, is the main source of the oxygen we breathe.

When Thor Heyerdahl crossed the Pacific in his raft *Kon-Tiki* in 1947 he was able to use the ocean water quite freely. When he crossed the Atlantic in the papyrus boat *Ra* in 1969 he said that almost all the way across the ocean there was nothing but rubbish.

According to Jan Thulin and Andris Andrushaitis, in 'The Baltic Sea under threat', a talk given to the Fifth Religion, Science and Environmental Symposium of the Ecumenical Patriarch in 2003, the Baltic Sea is seriously under threat from eutrophication (excessive nutrient content caused by fertiliser runoff, which increases algae growth and reduces the amount of oxygen available for other species). Toxic hydrogen sulphide has formed in its deeper regions and nearly a third of the bottom area is calculated to be 'dead' — that is, there is almost no animal or fish life there.

Steve Chapple, in an article on reefs in the *Reader's Digest*, says that they are home to at least 25 percent of all fish species. According to the U.S. Coral Reef Taskforce, coral reefs support 33 percent of marine fish species. Worldwide, half of all reefs have vanished due to warmer oceans, pollution, overfishing and the acidification of the oceans from the increase of carbon dioxide. The rest could be extinct by mid-century. Reefs hold back waves during hurricanes; provide a nursery for fish that feed a billion people and provide 200 million jobs in the fishing industry; are a home for plants that treat cancer, HIV and other diseases; and provide considerable income from tourist revenue.

In Europe and the U.S. between five and ten percent of all wells examined have nitrate levels higher than the recommended maximum of 45 milligrams per litre.

Around 40 percent of the world's people — 2.5 billion people — lack basic toilets and more than 1 billion have little or no access to renewable water resources. Some estimates attribute up to 80 percent of illnesses and one third of deaths in Latin America and the Caribbean to contaminated water. Waterborne diseases such as cholera and dysentery take tens of thousands of African lives each year and kill more people worldwide than anything else, including HIV/Aids. Some estimate that nearly 4 million people die each year from polluted water, the majority women and children from poor areas. According to the World Health Organisation, the 4 billion cases of diarrhoea each year are associated with lack of access to safe water. 1.7 million people, mainly children under five, will die as a result. A 2010 report by the UN Environmental Programme says that more than half the world's hospital beds are occupied by people suffering from illnesses linked to contaminated water.

Since 1850, the extent of technology's reach has been so great that the planet's plumbing has been comprehensively reconfigured. In the twentieth century, using ancient and modern methods, several million dams, tube wells, canals, aqueducts and pipelines were built to divert water. In dry lands this has caused problems as fast as it has solved them. In the developing world only 53 percent of the population currently has access to good drinking water. According to *Sharing God's Planet; a*

Christian vision for a sustainable future, a report from the Mission and Public Affairs Council of the Anglican Church, UK, within six years more than 40 percent of the world's most vulnerable will suffer from water shortages. An estimated 75 to 250 million Africans are projected to face a water shortage by 2020, according to the Evangelical Environmental Network. Absorption of rainwater by eroded soils may be reduced by over 90 percent, resulting in water shortages even during years with good rainfall.

Overfishing

Cod fishing was banned off the coast of Newfoundland in 1992 following a collapse of the fishery. Recently it was reported that there is still no sign of recovery. Similar stories come from the North Sea, Japan and many other places. The European population of eels is one percent of that in 1980. Their American cousins are doing little better.

Forests

Over 1.6 billion people rely on forests for their livelihoods.

Sir Ghillean Prance, at the Regent College Creation Groaning Conference, declared that 50 percent of the total rainforest in the world was destroyed during the last half of the last century. Forests cover seven percent of the world's land area, yet contain half of the total species of plants and animals. 150 of the prescription drugs used in the U.S. come from plants, fungi and bacteria found in those rainforests. According to the World Health Organisation 60 percent of the world's population rely on plants for primary health care. The cutting and burning of forests accounts for 20 percent of the carbon dioxide released into the atmosphere. Flooding in places such as Bangladesh, Philippines and Mozambique is caused by forest destruction.

Cattle-ranching to feed the appetites of Europe and North America is a major cause of the destruction of the Amazonian rainforest, where it is estimated that a pound of beef 'costs' 200 square feet of rainforest.

According to the World Evangelical Theological Commission, forest cover in Thailand declined from 29 to 19 percent of the land area between 1985 and 1988. In the Philippines undisturbed forests have been reduced from 16 million hectares in 1960 to less than one million hectares. In

Ecuador since 1960 the original rainforest has been almost totally eliminated and the land used for cash crops: a small remnant at Rio Palenque of less than one square kilometre is the only remaining site for 43 plant species and the adjacent Centinella Ridge that once supported 100 endemic plant species was cleared between 1980 and 1984.

Steven Bouma-Prediger says that at least 200 million hectares of forest vanished between 1980 and 1995 alone — an area larger than Mexico. Cutting and burning forests in the 1980s released more carbon into the atmosphere than the rest of the world's forests absorbed. According to Calvin DeWitt in a primer sheet 'Creation Watch', tropical forests are currently destroyed at the rate of 25 million acres each year. Norman Myers, in *Nature's Services*, puts the total at 37 million acres per year. Other research suggests even higher rates. George Miller, in *Living in the Environment: Principles, connections, and solutions*, puts it at 75 million acres per year.

Molly O'Meara, in 'Harnessing Information Technologies for the Environment', *State of the World 2000*, says that despite the use of computers, average per capita consumption of printing and writing paper in industrial countries shot up by 24 percent between 1988 and 1998.

In Jeremiah 18:14 the permanence of the snow and waters of Lebanon is used as an illustration of the faithfulness of God. In Isaiah 35:1,2 the glory of Lebanon is a symbol of the future productivity of the nation and the glory of the people of God. In Psalm 92:12 we are told that '**the righteous ... will grow like a cedar of Lebanon.**' For the last decade the snow has been melting every summer and the springs are drying up. The hills are mostly barren, deforested generations ago and overgrazed by goats. The Litani River, the largest in Lebanon, is now a stagnant, toxic soup during most of the year. Cedars are reduced to twelve scattered fragments, two percent of their former area. Isaiah once foretold the rejoicing of his people, and nature itself, at God's judgement on the destructive nation of Babylon. '**All the lands are at rest and at peace; they break into singing. Even the junipers and cedars of Lebanon exult over you and say, "Now that you have been laid low, no one comes to cut us down"**' (Isaiah 14:7,8). Unfortunately that rejoicing has been short-lived.

Forest destruction is not just due to logging. Charles Little, in *Dying of the Trees*, writes of a growing list of human actions that so modify the environment that tree death and forest decline eventuate:

> Too much ground-level ozone and not enough stratospheric ozone; acidified soils over vast forest regions; a pattern of nutrient loss and an excess of other nutrients, such as nitrogen, that prove toxic; the deposition of heavy metals — cadmium, lead, copper, zinc, mercury — and the mobility of poisonous aluminium normally locked in the soil; the loss of beneficial mycorrhizal fungus; the destructive edge effects of clearcutting; the genetic weakness of replacement trees in impacted ecosystems; a host of plagues and diseases anxious to take advantage of the debilitated trees and forests; the unwanted effects of too-rapid climate change.

The five countries with the largest rainforest areas are also among the world's most heavily indebted countries, therefore placing them under tremendous pressure to cut and clear rainforests to finance repayments.

Zoologist Andrew Balmford, whose work resulted in the great leap forward of conservation research made recently at Cambridge University with the founding of three new chairs, demonstrated a few years ago that habitat destruction costs the world the equivalent of US$250 billion a year.

Hunger and poverty

Steven Bouma-Prediger says that, lined up shoulder to shoulder, the world's hungry would stretch around the planet 18 times. The latest figure from UN's Food and Agriculture Organisation say there are now 1 billion hungry people in the world. This is expected to double by 2050. The World Food Programme reports that one child dies of hunger every six seconds.

Sir Ghillean Prance says that the poorest 20 percent control only 1.4 percent of the total production of wealth. 1.4 billion people still live on less than US$1.25 a day according to the recently updated poverty line. The World Bank has predicted that more than 5 billion people will earn less than $2 a day in income by 2030, and 2 billion of them will live in slums in dozens of cities with populations greater than 10 million.

It is often women who suffer most when clean drinking water, fuel and healthy surroundings are not available. When the earth is damaged, it is the poor who suffer, time and time again.

Animal and plant extinctions

According to the Official Video of the International Year of Biodiversity (2010), hosted by Ban Ki-Moon, 6.5 billion people are sustained by ecosystems containing almost two million known species, though there could be 90 million unknown species. Twelve percent of birds are threatened with extinction, 21 percent of mammals, 28 percent of reptiles, 30 percent of amphibians, 35 percent of invertebrates, 37 percent of freshwater fish and 70 percent of plants. Invasive species, introduced by humans, are responsible for 40 percent of all animal species extinctions of which the cause is known. By 2006 over 200 dead zones in lakes and seas were caused by pesticides and fertiliser runoff. Unsustainable use has led to three quarters of the world's lakes and seas being overexploited or despoiled. Half of the world's wetlands have been drained.

According to a report published by Scientists from the Botanical Gardens at Kew, London's Natural History Museum and the International Union for the Conservation of Nature, 'The single greatest threat is conversion of natural habitats to agricultural use, directly impacting 33 percent of threatened species'.

Humans have driven 15 percent of the earth's species to extinction in the last 100 years.

DeWitt, in 'Creation Watch', estimates that a scientifically reasonable figure for current extinctions is three a day. Archaeological evidence suggests that the rate of extinctions before humans came on the scene was much lower. However, well-respected biologists E O Wilson, Paul Ehrlich, and Peter Raven have recently put the extinction rate much higher still — more like 50 to 150 species a day in the tropical rainforests. According to the Official Video of the International Year of Biodiversity cited above, something like 130 species are becoming extinct daily, which is 1000 times the natural extinction rate. According to the World Conservation Union's 1996 global survey, approximately 66 percent of the world's bird species are in decline, with 11 percent of all birds threatened with extinction.

Of the 2400 birds, reptiles and plants on the threatened list in New Zealand, 800 are in acute or chronic decline and no work is targeted to protect 616 of them.

Sir Ghillean Prance reported that in the last 30 years there has been an alarming decline in frogs and other amphibians in places as far apart as Australia and Costa Rica. Many frogs are born with multiple legs and other deformities. Amphibians are particularly susceptible to UV radiation. According to Paul Hawken in *Blessed Unrest*, when tadpoles are exposed to the pesticide Atrazine at 1/30,000th of 'safe' levels, 20 percent of them become hermaphroditic and sterile adults. Infinitesimal chemical exposure during development can have a drastically different effect from that at maturity.

Prance says, 'The current rate of extinction, caused by humans, is at least a thousand times more than the natural rate of extinction. Climate change is now the biggest threat to biodiversity.'

Aldo Leopold expressed well in his essay 'The Round River', 'If the biota, in the course of aeons, has built something we like but do not understand, then who but a fool would discard seemingly useless parts? To keep every cog and wheel is the first precaution of intelligent tinkering.'

Studies of more than one thousand species of plants, animals, and insects found an average migration rate toward the north and south poles of about four miles per decade in the second half of the twentieth century due to global warming. This is not fast enough. During the past 30 years, the lines marking regions in which a given average temperature prevails (isotherms), have been moving poleward at a rate of about 35 miles per decade.

Based on the proportion of twenty-first-century carbon dioxide emissions provided by one large coal-fired power plant over its lifetime, James Hansen estimates that a single power plant should be assigned responsibility for exterminating about 400 species.

There have been five mass extinctions during the past 500 million years — geologically brief periods in which about half or more of the species on earth disappeared forever. Enough is now known to provide an invaluable perspective for what is already being called the sixth mass extinction, the human-caused destruction of species.

Air pollution

John McNeil, in *Something New under the Sun,* says, 'Urban air pollution dates from earlier times but in the twentieth century reached levels sufficient to kill, it is suggested, somewhere between 25 and 40 million people through respiratory disease.'

Acid rain

According to Bill McKibben in *The End of Nature,* all bodies of fresh water in Sweden are now acidic, with 'roughly fifteen thousand of them too sour to support life.' The rain in Europe is roughly 10 to 14 times more acidic than normal. 50 percent of all trees in Germany are affected by acid rain.

E G Nisbet, in *Leaving Eden: To Protect and Manage the Earth,* says that in the Adirondacks of upstate New York approximately one-quarter of the 2759 lakes and ponds are fishless because of acid deposition or have been damaged to the point at which fish populations have been substantially reduced. Acid rain is a global problem, with virtually no region untouched by its effects.

Topsoil erosion

Ronald Sider, in 'Redeeming the Environment', in *Christianity Today,* says that in the last 40 years the earth has lost one-fifth of its topsoil.

According to George Miller in *Living in the Environment,* the average amount of topsoil lost per hectare annually in the U.S., due to wind, and more particularly water, is 18 tonnes. Worldwide annual erosion rates for farmland are 20 to 100 times the natural renewal rate.

Desertification

Miller says that in the last 50 years desert areas of the earth have increased by an area the size of Brazil. 60,000 square kilometres are added annually. This can occur from natural causes, but is also due to overgrazing, cultivation of marginal land, deforestation and other human practices.

We have the same impact on the earth in five minutes that our ancestors in 5000 BC had in a year. Surely what Paul Hawken states is true: 'Although the scale of environmental and social breakdown is so vast it isn't possible for any one individual or institution to be fully informed about it, the warning signs are omnipresent.'

CHAPTER 2

Causes of the problem

The causes of all this devastation are multiple. The following reasons are those I consider most significant.

Ignorance

Despite all our scientific progress, we actually undesrtand very little about the complexity and interrelatedness of ecosystems and the harm we do by many of our actions. The world is more complex than we can possibly imagine. To give an example, Dr Martin Ellwood, a Research Fellow at Trinity Hall, Cambridge, says:

> We have identified fewer than 20% of the insect species, even though insects are some of the most ecologically important animals on Earth. We have virtually no idea how insect diversity, or indeed the diversity of any organisms, is generated and maintained. In the face of our planet's worst extinction crisis, resolving this issue represents one of the most urgent but also one of the most exciting goals of modern ecology.

Too often this ignorance has been inexcusable. Paul Wachtel, in *The Poverty of Affluence: A psychological portrait of the American way of life*, speaks of 'pollution and the problem of environmental limits' as 'the weightiest of all the denied realities of the consumer life'.

Numerous examples could be cited where humans have upset the balance of nature that has developed over millions of years, often with devastating consequences. This has often happened by transferring a species to a new environment, with good intentions but with harmful effects on the host environment, or by seeking to eradicate a species thought to be harmful in a certain area, while ignorant of its other benefits. Probably one of the greatest causes of the extinction of species worldwide is the introduction of alien species, whether plants, animals or insects. Even when complete environmental impact studies are carried out, disasters can occur.

The urgency of education about those things we do know is vital. I agree with eco-feminist Heather Eaton, who writes, 'If … the natural world [is] invisible in our education, [its] destruction will be as well.' Surely it is as important as reading, writing and arithmetic? The earlier we can start with our children, the better.

Economic materialism

Douglas Meeks, in *God the Economist: The doctrine of God and political economy*, argues that money displaces God as the ordering force or guiding spirit of modern relations of exchange and of modern culture. Or as Donald Worster puts it in *The Wealth of Nature: Environmental history and the ecological imagination*, 'worshipping the god of the GNP.' He writes that we inhabit a culture in which

> improving one's physical condition — i.e., achieving more comfort, more bodily pleasure, and especially higher levels of affluence — is the greatest good in life, greater than securing the salvation of one's soul, greater than learning reverence for nature or God.

Worster critiques the usual cast of suspects — Descartes, Francis Bacon — but nominates Adam Smith as 'the representative modern man, the most complete embodiment of that cultural shift' called materialism. In his famous tome *The Wealth of Nations* Smith argued (as Locke before him) that the natural world has no intrinsic value irrespective of its usefulness to humans. Worster reminds us that

> the human economy requires for its long-term success that its architects acknowledge their dependence on the greater economy of nature, preserving its health and respecting its benefits. By this standard every modern economy, whether built on the principles of Adam Smith or Karl Marx, is an unmitigated disaster.

Bob Goudzwaard, in *Capitalism and Progress: A diagnosis of Western society*, Brian Walsh and Richard Middleton, in *The Transforming Vision*, and Alan Miller, in *Gaia Connections*, also point to a misplaced faith in economic prosperity, or 'economism', as one of the leading factors in ecological despoliation. John Maynard Keynes cautioned that we live our lives under the illusion of freedom but are likely to be 'slaves to some defunct economist.' And as Paul Hawken says, 'There can be no sustainability when institutions whose primary purpose is to create money are dictating the standards.'

The modern economy has made possible the untrammelled expression of greed and pride of possession by an ever-larger proportion of humanity. Christopher Wright, in *The Mission of God: Unlocking the Bible's grand narrative*, spells out the problem very clearly:

> There is no doubt that a major contributor to contemporary environmental damage is global capitalism's insatiable demand for 'more.' It is not only in the private sphere that the biblical truth is relevant that covetousness is idolatry and the love of money is the root of all kinds of evil, including this one. There is greed for
>
> - minerals and oil, at any cost;
> - land to graze cattle and birds, to meet obscene human fashions in clothes, toys, ornaments, and aphrodisiacs;
> - commercial or tourist exploitation of fragile and irreplaceable habitats;
> - market domination through practices that produce the goods at least cost to the exploiter and maximum cost to the country and people exploited.

The motto of the native Hawaiians in the state park on the Island of Kaua'I is, 'The life of the land, is perpetuated in righteousness.'

We cannot escape the fact that in today's world, so much of what we do has its effect on somebody else. In the words of George Miller, every one of us is downwind or downstream of everyone else. For Garrett Hardin in *Filters Against Folly*, this is 'the first law of ecology'. And as Henry David Thoreau said many years ago, 'Most of the luxuries, and many of the so-called comforts of life, are not only indispensable, but positive hindrances to the elevation of mankind.'

Even the most remote villages of Africa, Asia and Latin America feel the effects of decisions made by the World Trade Organisation, the World Bank, the International Monetary Fund, multinational corporations, and the governments of stronger nations. 'Eco-justice' is a recent and very necessary word in our dictionary. We need to be reminded constantly of what the local environment means to the poor. Dr Stella Simiyu, a Kenyan botanist and member of A Rocha* International Council of Reference, puts it like this:

> The rural poor depend directly on the natural resource base. This is where their pharmacy is, this is where their supermarket is, this is in fact their fuel station, their power company, their water company. What would happen to you if these things were removed from your local neighbourhood? Therefore we really cannot afford not to invest in environmental conservation.

Such is the motive power of profit that risks are taken with nature that may threaten human health or non-human species diversity. And as the free market's most articulate defender, *New York Times* columnist Thomas Friedman, acknowledges in *The Lexus and the Olive Tree*:

> The hidden hand of the market will never work without a hidden fist. McDonalds cannot flourish without McDonnell Douglas. And the hidden fist that keeps the world safe for Silicon Valley's technologies to flourish is called the U.S. Army, Air Force, Navy and Marine Corps.

The consumer society that emerged in eighteenth-century England has grown to massive proportions with the advance of technology and communication. 'We are held captive by dissatisfaction,' writes Mary Jo Leddy in *Radical Gratitude*. As a consequence, 'Ingratitude is ingrained within every social class within the culture of money. It is how sin takes shape within us, conditions us, and hold us captive.'

Wendell Berry, in his insightful book *Sex, Economy, Freedom & Community*, is blunt about the harmful effects of an overemphasis on economic growth:

> The aims of productivity, profitability, efficiency, limitless growth, limitless wealth, limitless power, limitless mechanisation and

---

*   A Christian environmental organisation.

automation can enrich and empower the few (for a while), but they will sooner or later ruin us all. The gross national product and the corporate bottom line are utterly meaningless as measures of the prosperity or health of the country … The true source and analogue of our economic life is the economy of plants, which never exceeds natural limits, never grows beyond the power of its place to support it, produces no waste, and enriches and preserves itself by death and decay.

He suggests the following values necessary for a healthy society:

We must learn to prefer quality over quantity, service over profit, neighbourliness over competition, people and other creatures over machines, health over wealth, a democratic prosperity over centralised wealth and power, economic health over 'economic growth'.

Researchers at the University of British Columbia estimated that it would take four earths' worth of productive land to enable all the world's people to consume resources at the rate of North Americans. It would take ten planets to absorb the greenhouse gases being pumped aloft. All this is in spite of some excellent studies that point to the lack of connection between affluence and happiness. Louis Harris, in *The Anguish of Change*, has pointed out that, in Sweden, 'advances in human welfare associated with economic growth came to a halt in the mid-1960s while alienation, boredom at work, mental illness, social tension, suicides, alcoholism and loneliness kept increasing.' Social psychologist David Myers, after an extensive review of relevant literature, concluded that there was no correlation whatever between wealth and well-being. In *The Pursuit of Happiness* he says: 'Our becoming much better-off over the last 30 years has not been accompanied by one iota of increased happiness and life satisfaction.'

John Kenneth Galbraith, in *The Affluent Society*, predicted the 'private affluence and public squalor' that has come to characterise the social ecology of many modern societies.

As Albert Einstein declared:

Not until the creation and maintenance of decent conditions of life for all people are recognised and accepted as a common obligation of all people and all countries — not until then shall

we, with a certain degree of justification, be able to speak of
humankind as civilised.

The growth of resource-hungry corporations

Decisions are made in boardrooms far removed from local sources
of production. There is the unspoken view that capital has a right to
grow, a right greater that the rights of communities and cultures. Local
communities that have lived sustainably with nature for generations lose
control over the production of their needs. For example, the average item
of food in an American supermarket has travelled 1500 miles. The ease
with which food and commercial goods can be transported around the
world often undermines the sufficiency and economic stability of local
communities. Goods become of greater importance than people. Giving
control of the environment to local communities has often proved more
effective than centralised government or WWF schemes. The division
between environmental and social justice is an artificial one. How we treat
the earth will invariably affect others. Concerns about water, climate, soil
and biodiversity are inseparable from concerns about worker health, living
wages, equity, education, and basic human rights. Paul Hawken, in his
book *Blessed Unrest*, says, 'No culture has ever honoured its environment
but disgraced its people, and conversely, no government can say it cares
for its citizens while allowing the environment to be trashed.' Arthur
Paul Boers, in *Lord, Teach Us to Pray*, says, 'Woe, woe, to the persons or
institutions or economic systems that keep people hungry. They stand
between the God-given gift of food and God's intended recipients!'

The global greenhouse gas emissions of British multinational
companies exceed all emissions within Britain itself many times over.
Though many corporations emit more carbon than many nation-states,
under the Kyoto Protocol they are not required to reduce their emissions
in parallel with nation-states.

The world's top 200 companies have twice the assets of 80 percent of
the world's people, and that asset base is growing 50 times faster than the
income of the world's majority.

Holms Ralston, in his important book *Philosophy Gone Wild* (1989)
argues that we have a duty to 'stabilise the ecosystem through mutually
imposed self-limited growth.' Pioneer conservationist Aldo Leopold

put it this way: 'A thing is right when it tends to preserve the integrity, stability and the beauty of the biotic community. It is wrong when it tends otherwise.'

Jesus taught us to pray only for the needs of each day (Matthew 6:11). Those who tried hoarding the manna given by God in the wilderness found that it bred maggots and stank (Exodus 16:20). John Taylor, in *Enough is Enough*, comments: 'It is this stink which rises today from all over our despoiled environment.'

Putting humans centre stage in place of God

The Bible speaks of the value of creation because of God's delight in it and because it reveals his glory. Modern thinking has changed all this. As Philip Sampson states in 'A natural mistake' in *The Third Way*:

> It was the Enlightenment that reverted to Greek thinking and transformed dominion into domination, stewardship into anthropomorphism, and creation into 'Our environment'. It is the modern conception that humans live within 'an environment' that sets us at the centre of the world — and this is an Enlightenment story, not a Bible one.

Michael Northcott, in *A Moral Climate,* adds a consequence of this:

> The refusal to recognise moral or ecological constraints to mercantile and technological power is also a part of the legacy of the European Enlightenment and the modern struggle for emancipation from the authority of the church, tradition and faith, as well as from nature. But the paradox is that in the course of this emancipation nature *and* society are increasingly dominated by technological power. Dietrich Bonhoeffer suggested that it is because of the modern rationalism, science and technology train modern humans not to see the earth as a divine creation. Consequently 'the earth is no longer our earth, and then we become strangers on earth', and from strangers we finally become earth's subjects: through the power of technology 'the earth grips man and subdues him'.*

---

*   *Creation and Fall: A Theological Interpretation of Genesis 1–3*, ed. John W De Gruchy, translated by Douglas Stephen Bax.

Commenting on the decaying monuments of empires, such as the tower of Babylon, the ziggurats of Iraq, the Great Wall of China and the amphitheatre and aqueducts of Rome, Northcott says:

> The ruin of these monuments is indicative of the judgement that awaits those civilisations which have sought to replace the Creator with the work of human hands, and to substitute centrally stored wealth for the reliance upon the regenerative capacities of local ecosystems.

When God set up humans in the Garden of Eden, though providing them with abundance, he did set limits on their use of the available resources (Genesis 2:16,17). Modern humans, leaving God out of the picture, see themselves as autonomous, accountable to none but themselves, and consequently only recognise limits enforced by other humans.

An unhealthy reliance on human reason

The excessive trust we place in our own human wisdom — that however great the problems, we will find a solution — is undoubtedly a major factor in the environmental problems we have created. Dave Bookless, in *Planetwise,* aptly calls this the '*Titanic* syndrome'. We have forgotten that '**The fear of the Lord is the beginning of knowledge**' (Proverbs 1:7). As C S Lewis put it, if we leave God out of the picture, we are left with cold science or sloppy sentiment. Worster is right when he declares:

> The ecological crisis we have begun to experience in recent years is fast becoming the crisis of modern culture, calling into question not only the ethos of the marketplace or industrialism but also the central story that we have been telling ourselves over the past two or three centuries; the story of man's triumph by reason over the rest of nature.

Under this heading we could also include an over-reliance on science where science has been set over against nature as has happened in much thinking over the last few centuries. Northcott puts it in *The Environment and Christian Ethics:*

> Nature is available for human expropriation and exploitation. Indeed, without the application of human rationality and order, nature is perceived in the classical scientific paradigm as

unproductive and meaningless. Nature is said to have no purpose other than that which humans impute to it.

In 1974 Edward Goldsmith and the editors of *The Ecologist* put out a famous manifesto, which was endorsed by a score of Britain's most eminent biologists. In words that have been largely unheeded they stated:

> To suppose that we can assure the functioning of the ecosphere ourselves, with the sole aid of technological devices, thereby dispensing with the elaborate set of self-regulating mechanisms that has taken thousands of millions of years to evolve is an absurd piece of anthropocentric presumption that belongs to the realm of pure fantasy.

Philip Sherrard, in *Rape of Man and Nature*, argues that the scientist has taken the place of the priest, bringing to birth a new kind of society oriented towards consumerism rather than the eucharistic worship of God.

> For Herbert Spencer and the social Darwinists, the theory of natural selection was used to emphasise the superiority of humans with a consequent downgrading of the rest of nature. This ideology was used to legitimise the alterations and destruction of nature that humans brought about through industrialisation and technology.

And as C S Lewis explains in *The Abolition of Man*, the human conquest of nature brings about the rejection of the idea that goodness and virtue are part of the structure of the universe as has been commonly believed by Platonists, Confucians, Christians and Hindus alike.

Though science and technology are, in themselves, morally neutral, and can serve both good and bad purposes, the advances over the last century have made possible the destruction of nature on an alarming scale.

Fortunately, belief in continued and unlimited economic and technological progress as the chief means of improving the quality of life for the human race is beginning to change in Western societies, though it is not changing fast enough.

Migration to large cities

It seems as if the increased rate of destruction of the earth's ecosystems has coincided to some extent with the migration of rural communities to large cities, where human business, noise and lack of connection with nature shuts out the voice of God in creation. As Wendell Berry suggests in *Standing by Words*, when people cease to be involved in the kinds of work which sustain human dwelling and the fertility of the earth, they also lose touch with the 'perennial and substantial world in which we really do live'.

Monoculture

The continuing impact of monocropping in both forestry (which began in the eighteenth century as it was considered to be more 'efficient' than diverse natural forest) and commercial agriculture is the principle cause of the loss of species diversity, both in the developed and developing worlds. History affords a significant warning of the dangers of monoculture in the Irish famine of 1845, the worst human disaster to hit Europe since the Black Death of the Middle Ages. One threat common to other crops at the time was the increasing concentration on a smaller number of varieties. The Irish became dependant on a single potato variety. While the potato blight hit other parts of Europe it was devastating in Ireland because of this monoculture. Disease spreads much more easily and quickly where plants are all of one species. A diverse forest, by contrast, produces more timber, sustains healthier soil and recycles more carbon dioxide.

War

Those who have seen battle scenes of France and Germany during the two world wars or remember news footage of whole segments of lush jungles in Vietnam destroyed by napalm will know something of the devastation war can cause.

The rise of nation states in thirteenth-century Europe and the consequent growth of state bureaucracies and standing armies increased the demand for finance to support wars. This created a money economy, which has proved increasingly unfriendly to the environment. This, in turn, put pressure on more sustainable methods of farming.

For every dollar spent on UN peacekeeping, $2000 is spent on war-making by member nations. Four of the five members of the UN Security Council, which has veto power over all UN resolutions, are the top weapons dealers in the world: the United States, the United Kingdom, France and Russia.

The noted anthropologist Loren Eiseley lamented the losses in the 'natural' world caused by humans, and spoke darkly of the future in *The Firmament of Time*:

> It is with the coming of man that a vast hole seems to open in nature, a vast black whirlpool spinning faster and faster, consuming flesh, stones, soil, minerals, sucking down the lightning, wrenching power from the atom, until the ancient sounds of nature are drowned in the cacophony of something which is no longer nature, something instead which is loose and knocking at the world's heart, something demonic …

And as U Utah Phillips reminds us: 'The Earth is not dying — it is being killed. And the people who are killing it have names and addresses.'

CHAPTER 3

The modern environmental movement

Though there were significant environmentalists at an earlier date, such as George Marsh and John Muir in the nineteenth century, the modern environmental movement could be said to have emerged in the early 1960s, prompted by Rachel Carson's book *Silent Spring*, by growing concern over nuclear war and nuclear testing, and by widespread awareness of the damage caused by post-war population and technology growth. Carson was a renowned nature author and marine biologist with the U.S. Fish and Wildlife Service. In 1939 she wrote to the *Reader's Digest* proposing an article about a series of tests being conducted on DDT, the most powerful pesticide the world has ever known. The magazine rejected the idea. *Silent Spring*, published in 1962, took four years of thorough research to complete. She finished it while suffering severely from cancer. She was able to show how DDT entered the food chain and had contaminated the entire world's food supply, causing cancer and genetic damage. Anticipating the indignation of the chemical industry, which questioned her integrity and even her sanity, she had compiled 55 pages of notes and a list of experts who had read and approved the manuscript. Typical of what she had to cope with was the following letter to *The New Yorker*:

> Miss Rachel Carson's reference to the selfishness of insecticide manufacturers probably reflects her Communist sympathies, like a lot of writers these days. We can live without birds and animals, but, as the current market slump shows, we cannot live without business. As for insects, isn't it just like a woman to be scared to death of little bugs! As long as we have the H-bomb everything will be OK.
>
> P. S. She's probably a peace-nut too.

Her book had two significant effects. Firstly, as Paul Hawken points out:

> Her exposé of industry-sponsored poisoning of the environment brought for the first time a broad cross section of the population into the environmental dialogue. The environment now included people's bodies, mothers' milk, African Americans, farmworkers, and the poor, some of whom were just as polluted as the Cuyahoga River, which famously caught fire in 1969.

Secondly:

> *Silent Spring* ended a century-long accommodation between industry and the environment, enlarging the conceptual framework of the environmental movement from conservation to include human rights and the rights of all living beings.

One month after giving her final speech in 1963, shortly before she died, five million dead fish floated to the surface of the lower Mississippi river.

The book alarmed readers across America and for the first time the need to control the activities of industry in order to protect the environment became widely accepted. When President Kennedy ordered his advisory committee to examine the issues the book raised, its report thoroughly vindicated both *Silent Spring* and its author.

On 22 April 1970, the first Earth Day, 20 million Americans went onto the streets and into the parks and auditoriums to demonstrate for a healthy, sustainable environment. Thousands of colleges and universities organised protests against the deterioration of the environment. Groups that had been fighting against oil spills, polluting factories and power plants, raw sewerage, toxic dumps, pesticides, freeways, the loss of wilderness and the extinction of wildlife suddenly realised that they had common values. This led to the creation of the United States Environmental Protection Agency and the passage of the Clean Air Act, the Clean Water Act, and the Endangered Species Act.

In 1987, a UN report of the Commission on Environment and Development, 'Our common future', explained that a healthy planet and a healthy population together make up one goal, not two. Humans will not prosper if the earth languishes.

In 1990 Earth Day went global, mobilising 200 million people in 141 countries and lifting the status of environmental issues to the world stage.

This helped pave the way for the 1992 United Nations Earth Summit in Rio. This was the first time the entire global community had gathered to discuss environmental issues. Then UN Secretary-General Boutros-Ghali, summing up the impact of the Rio Summit, stated it is

> no longer enough for man to love his neighbour; he must now love the world. Beyond man's covenant with God and his social contract with his fellowmen, we now need an ethical contract with nature and the earth ... The earth has a soul. To restore it is the essence of Rio.

In 1997, the International Conference on Climate Change took place in Kyoto, Japan. There, developed countries agreed to specific targets for cutting their emissions of greenhouse gases. A general framework was defined for this, with specifics to be detailed over the next few years. This became known as the Kyoto Protocol. Industrialised countries were committed to an overall reduction of emissions of greenhouse gases to 5.2 percent below 1990 levels for the period 2008–12. (The Intergovernmental Panel on Climate Change said in its 1990 report that a 60 percent reduction in emissions was needed).

The 2002 Johannesburg World Summit on Sustainable Development was a watershed. Despite much optimism at the Rio Summit and huge efforts in preceding years, there had been little progress, largely because people did not want to give up their polluting lifestyles. Johannesburg saw a call for the world's faith communities to get involved, recognising that religions know something about changing people's inner motivation. As an example the WWF started a programme called 'Sacred Gifts for a Living Planet', stating that it was 'encouraging the faiths to enlarge the significant role they play in caring for the environment.'

Conservation organisations such as the Nature Conservancy, the WWF, the National Wildlife Federation and the National Geographical Society are well funded. As of 2005, the Nature Conservancy had $1.7 billion in liquid assets and $4.4 billion in total assets. These organisations are not threatening to the establishment because they *are* the establishment. They are effective and have a lot of clout.

This century, business, national and international conferences on the environment have proliferated. On 6 July 2009, the 7th International Conference on the Environment and Sustainable Development: Creating

Awareness to Save the Planet was held in Havana, Cuba. The wwf says the only nation living sustainably is Cuba.

One thing is very plain from the events of the last 50 years — we can't leave it to politicians to make the necessary changes. Such advances that have been made have come from the mobilising of ordinary, highly motivated people with the backing of many in the scientific community. A handful of high-profile people have achieved much, such as Al Gore and his powerful documentary *An Inconvenient Truth*. However, even he emphasises that significant changes will only come from a mass grass-roots movement.

All over the world environmental communities of all shapes and sizes are taking root, as people no longer trust the universalising values of the trader, the miner, the accountant, the planner and the government lawyer to protect their local environment. Paul Hawken estimated in 2007 that there were likely over 2 million organisations working toward ecological sustainability and social justice worldwide. That could be considerably higher now. The website he initiated, www.wiserearth.org, lists thousands of them. If we know where to look we may be encouraged, though he says, 'As yet there has been no coming together of organisations in a united front that can counter the massive scale and power of the global corporations and lobbyists that protect the status quo.'

Let's take courage from those responsible for the legal abolition of the slave trade. All social justice organisations can trace their origins back some 220 years ago, when three-quarters of the world were enslaved in one form or another. In 1787 a dozen people began meeting in a small print shop in London to abolish the lucrative slave trade. In spite of incredible opposition and ridicule from businessmen and politicians, six decades later slavery was outlawed almost everywhere.

CHAPTER 4

The positive and negative influence of Christianity

An intriguing article by Lynn White, Jr., a professor of History at the University of California, 'The historical roots of our ecological crisis', was published in *Science* magazine in 1967. This provoked a furious controversy and has been quoted and debated ever since. It is still found in almost every environmental philosophy, theology, and ethics anthology and referred to in virtually every textbook. Some have found in his analysis a justification for seeing the church as the planet's enemy. In it he stated rightly that 'human ecology is deeply conditioned by beliefs about our nature and destiny — that is religion.' However, he tended to blame Christianity above all other religions for the mess we are in. He states that the destructive effects of modern technology, 'the population explosion, the carcinoma of planless urbanism, the new geological deposits of sewerage and garbage' are 'at least partly to be explained … as a realisation of the Christian dogma of man's transcendence of, and rightful mastery over, nature.' Christianity, he insisted, told people that humans had a *right* to dominate nature, and it was therefore 'the most anthropocentric religion in the world.' Since the publication of this article, the idea of blaming Christians for the environmental crisis has attracted a wide range of committed defenders. However, one positive effect of White's essay was to galvanise some Christians to action.

Though we must be prepared to acknowledge what truth there is in White's claims, his article reveals certain imbalances, which are well summed up by James Nash in *Loving Nature*. He argues that White tends

to reduce the explanation of the complex ecological crisis to
a single cause, to exaggerate the authority of Christianity in
cultures, to minimise the fact that non-Christian cultures also
have been environmental despoilers, to overlook a number of
dissenting opinions in Christian history, and to underestimate
the potential for ecological reform in Christianity.

In spite of the interpretations that have been put on the Bible by many
of its adherents, Christianity can well be described as 'a religion and
philosophy of creation', in contrast to other religions of the ancient world,
as Clarence Glacken states in his magisterial study of nature and culture
in Western thought, *Traces on the Rhodian Shore*. While not the central
message of scripture, Walsh and Middleton, in *The Transforming Vision*,
describe creation as 'the underlying foundation' without which 'our
understanding of both sin and redemption will inevitably be distorted.'
I trust this will be made plain when we look at what the Bible has to say
about the subject.

In *Travail of Nature* Paul Santmire clearly shows that in contrast to
certain unhelpful dualisms between spirit and matter that can be found in
Christianity, there stands the 'ecological motive' as one of the dominant
theological themes in Christian history.

There have been many inspiring examples of sustainable living and
creation care through church history, such as St Anthony, St Francis
of Assisi, early Celtic Christianity, and Benedictine and Cistercian
monasticism in the Middle Ages. The early monastic communities were
models of sustainable farming, self-sufficiency and self-government,
reflecting the Hebrew and Christian vision of natural stewardship and
pastoralism, until later corrupted by increasing wealth. Nature was a
gift, not property, for land belonged absolutely to God, not humans. The
offices of prayer, together with holy days and Sundays, set a pattern
of work, contemplation and recreation which regulated work and
economy. Usury was wrong because it allowed financial debt to become
the ordering principle of human relations and real human needs. It is
examples such as these that prompted Robin Attfield to conclude, 'Belief
in man's stewardship is far more ancient and has been far more consistent
among Christians than the assaults of critics would suggest.'

Other significant names from the past in matters of ecology are the Swedish botanist Linnaeus (1707–78), arguably the greatest natural historian of the Enlightenment; William Carey, the nineteenth-century Baptist missionary to India; and John Muir (1838–1914), whose letters, essays and books have been read by millions and are still read today. Many more examples could be given.

The campaign against cruelty to animals grew out of the Christian conviction that humans should care for God's creation. Luther, for example, found in the Bible that we have to be merciful to animals and protect them and that we shall give an account for any mistreatment of them and that the arbitrary killing of even wild beasts (such as for sport) is not permitted. Calvin's commentary on the Deuteronomic law against cruelty in farming is equally clear. The Puritans in England, Scotland and North America inherited and developed these insights. John Bulwer in the seventeenth century questioned whether it was lawful for humans to eradicate any species because this was 'taking away one link of God's chain, one note of his harmony.' Dissenters, Quakers, Evangelicals and Methodists of the eighteenth century also played an essential role. Arthur Broome, an evangelical clergyman, built on this foundation when he established the Society for the Prevention of Cruelty to Animals in 1824 with money from William Wilberforce. This was a long way from Aristotle's line that 'Nature has made all the animals for the sake of men.'

Negative influences of Christianity

However, not all has been well within the Christian faith. Tim Keller, who has had a very effective pastoral ministry in Manhattan's Upper East Side for over 20 years, has a significant word of advice for Christians when he points out that all human beings are equally formed by both the creation and the Fall: 'non-believers are far better than their wrong beliefs should make them, and we Christians are far worse than our beliefs should make us.' Wendell Berry, farmer, writer and academic, much of whose writing has a prophetic quality, describes our failings very plainly in *Sex, Economy, Freedom & Community*:

> Despite protests to the contrary, modern Christianity has become willy-nilly the religion of the state and the economic status quo. Because it has been so exclusively dedicated to

incanting anaemic souls into Heaven, it has been made the tool
of much earthly villainy. It has, for the most part, stood silently
by while a predatory economy has ravaged the world, destroyed
its natural beauty and health, divided and plundered its human
communities and households. It has flown the flag and chanted
the slogans of empire. It has assumed with the economists that
'economic forces' automatically work for good and has assumed
with the industrialists and militarists that technology determines
history. It has assumed with almost everybody that 'progress' is
good, that it is good to be modern and up with the times. It has
admired Caesar and comforted him in his depredations and
defaults. But in its de facto alliance with Caesar, Christianity
connives directly in the murder of Creation.

A significant problem that arose fairly early in Christian writings
was the influence of some Greek thinking, that tended to think of
matter as fundamentally evil. A growing ambiguity can be detected
in early Christian theologies about the nature of matter and human
bodies, and a growing disjunction between human salvation and the
corruptible creation. This shift can already be detected in the writings
of the influential fourth-century theologian and bishop, Athanasius of
Alexandria.

Richard Sennett, in *Conscience of the Eye*, suggests that there has
emerged in the West a tragic alienation between the inner spiritual
life and the outer material world which he rather tenuously traces to
Augustine, but which others trace to developments in medieval theology,
which reached full flowering after the Reformation. Also we could add
the tendency in early Protestant theology to emphasise the fallenness
of nature more strongly than their medieval forebears and treat nature
as a resource created entirely for human purposes. Richard Bentley, for
example, wrote that 'all things' were made 'principally for the benefit of
man.' Similarly, the Puritans emphasised the total moral corruption of
the natural order and the responsibility of humans to remake the world
and call nature back to its original goodness. Also, the Protestant work
ethic tended to legitimise the growing money economy, which regards
nature primarily as a resource for human productivity and has not proved
healthy for nature.

We could also mention the neglect of non-Western theological perspectives. Wesley Granberg-Michaelson, in *Ecology and Life*, states, 'The Western church has been theologically arrogant and inattentive as well as condescending toward non-Western Christian perspectives.' Asian, African and South American churches have much to share, which we neglect at our peril.

Despite the very significant and growing emphasis of Christians on caring for creation, there still linger some negative influences. One is the emphasis expressed by James Watt, the first Reagan-era Secretary of the Interior. In response to a question during discussion with a committee of the House of Representatives as to why his agency was acting contrary to its expressed mandate, Watt, a devout Christian, said, 'I do not know how many future generations we can count on before the Lord returns.' This contrasts with Luther's comment that if he knew the Lord was coming today, he would still go out and plant his apple tree. Dispensationalist Christians in particular tend to spend so much time focusing on end-time scenarios that they appear to have little time or interest left to ponder the state of creation today.

According to a 1994 study by James Guth and Lyman Kellstedt, 'How Green Is My Pulpit?', Christian congregations that show the greatest seriousness regarding the Bible and are the most committed to biblical inerrancy are the very same congregations that tend to be the least concerned about ecology. Robert Booth Fowler, in *The Greening of Protestant Thought,* finds attitudes ranging from indifference to outright hostility toward the environmentalist movement in the more extreme fundamentalist wing of American Protestantism. If anything, this shows the vital importance of good biblical interpretation. Hopefully, if similar studies were done now they might show beginnings of change.

Sadly, some Christians are more concerned with *how* God created the earth, and in particular in arguing against evolutionary scientists, than they are with our responsibility to revel in, nurture and sustain God's creation today.

Others shun the environmentalist movement because many involved in it do not hold Christian beliefs. British authors Robert Whelan, Joseph Kirwan and Paul Haffner, in *The Cross and the Rainforest: A Critique of Radical Green Spirituality,* disparage the Christian church's new focus on creation, by claiming that the larger environmentalist movement should not be embraced in any way, because it propagates false views of the world and humanity's place in it.

Catholic priest Robert Sirico, founder of the Acton Institute for the study of Religion and Liberty, says, 'Nature does not have a metaphysical right … to be preserved and adored for reasons other than its usefulness to God's human creatures.'

A Barna Group study in the U.S. that found widespread environmental concern among Christians also found that only about a third of active churchgoers have heard teaching or preaching on environmental issues in their churches.

As B K Cunningham, Warden of Westcott House, wrote, 'The fact is that many people require not one but two conversions which we may inadequately call from Nature to Grace, and then back again from Grace to Nature.' Or, as Berry says, 'Our predicament now, I believe, requires us to learn to read and understand the Bible in the light of the present fact of Creation.'

CHAPTER 5

The modern Christian emphasis on caring for creation

One of the first to highlight environmental concerns from the last generation was Francis Schaeffer, who published *Pollution and the Death of Man* in 1970. This was partly a response to Lynn White Jr. and presented a more biblical view. An even more substantial work that appeared in 1970 was Paul Santmire's *Brother Earth*. With remarkable biblical and theological thoroughness, he sketched an ethic of 'The created realm of God' and an 'Ethic of responsibility'.

The Au Sable Institute, headed by Calvin DeWitt, who calls the Bible an 'environmental handbook', has probably been the single most powerful force in bringing Christians together on environmental issues and hosts productive meetings of evangelical scientists and theologians from all over the world. The institute has been called God's gift to the church in the U.S. and prepares hundreds of undergraduate and graduate students for environmental careers worldwide.

The U.S. National Association of Evangelicals (NAE) has over the years drafted resolutions underlining our responsibility as earth-keepers. In 1970 the NAE asserted that those who 'thoughtlessly destroy a God-ordained balance in nature are guilty of sin against God's creation.' It is true, however, that the World Evangelical Fellowship has not been as vocal as its liberal counterparts in dealing with ecological issues.

In the early 1970s there were few evangelicals involved in world hunger. Today some of the best relief operations are done by these evangelicals. They did not just start handing out food. They got the best minds together, collected the biblical material, and carefully planned.

Christian missions and relief organisations have come to recognise that environmental and developmental needs are not only compatible but also inseparable.

In 1977, Calvin College assembled a team of evangelical scholars to address 'Christian stewardship of natural resources.' The result, *Earthkeeping: Christian Stewardship of Natural Resources*, was an important resource throughout much of the 1980s for Christians interested in the subject.

In 1983, the World Council of Churches Assembly in Vancouver, under the heading Justice, Peace and the Integrity of Creation, began a process of international, national and regional conferences, which concluded in 1990 with the issuing of a covenant for the Justice, Peace and Integrity of Creation, to which member churches of the World Council of Churches were called to commit themselves. The covenant emphasised that the creation is the gift of God, and this good gift is being destroyed by the interwoven threats of violence, genocide, injustice for the world's poor, the denial of human rights and the degradation of the environment. It included the significant statement, 'The integrity of creation has a social aspect which we recognise as peace with justice, and an ecological aspect which we recognise in the self-renewing, sustainable character of natural eco-systems.'

The Christian Environmental Council was formed in the '80s. The Oxford Declaration on Christian Faith and Economics was hammered out among Christians of widely differing economic persuasions in 1990. It stated, 'Economic systems must be shaped so that a healthy ecological system is maintained over time.' The Evangelical Environmental Network was formed in 1992 with notable evangelical leaders such as Richard Mouw, Jim Wallis, Ronald Sider and Calvin DeWitt on its advisory council. It has prompted serious engagement in ecological issues in a variety of ways. In 1993 a group of Christian leaders gathered in Chicago and drafted 'An evangelical declaration on the care of creation.' Modelled in spirit on the 1973 'Evangelical declaration on social responsibility' focusing on hunger, poverty and racism, it begins:

> As followers of Jesus Christ, committed to the full authority of the Scripture, and aware of the ways we have degraded creation, we believe that biblical faith is essential to the solution of our ecological problems.

Christians for Environmental Stewardship, the Christian Environmental Project, and the Christian Society of the Green Cross were among Christian organisations formed in the early '90s. Even organisations not known primarily for an emphasis on creation stewardship are focusing on environmental issues. The InterVarsity Christian Fellowship has declared, 'We're trying to get our people to think in terms of creation care at all levels of our ministry.'

A Rocha, a Christian environmental organisation, supported by such eminent people as John Stott and Sir Ghillean Prance, is doing excellent work in twenty countries around the world.

Susan Drake, a U.S. State Department negotiator who played a key role behind the scenes at the Rio Earth Summit, often against considerable opposition and spiritual struggle, said she was helped immeasurably throughout by the prayer support of Christians at her church.

Sir John Houghton, co-chair of the Intergovernmental Panel on Climate Change's working group, lead editor of the first three IPCC reports, professor of atmospheric physics at Oxford and founder of the Hadley Centre for Climate Prediction and Research, is an evangelical Christian. He was the primary speaker at the meeting which produced the Evangelical Climate Initiative document signed by 86 prominent members.

Many members of the Coalition for Christian Colleges and Universities now offer environmental science majors.

Over the last decade or so, environmentally focused Christian websites, church programmes and Christian-based organisations and initiatives have multiplied profusely. There have been a growing number of excellent articles in magazines such as *Christianity Today* and *Christianity*. The number of Christian websites, campaigns and initiatives focusing on climate change is staggering. Environmental activism has been described as 'the fastest-growing form of Christian ministry.'

So, let's explore what the Bible has to say. I believe this is the best place to find the motivation, encouragement and hope that will enable us to do a better job of caring for planet earth in the future.

CHAPTER 6

Lessons from Genesis 1

There is much that is hinted at in the opening chapters of Genesis that is expounded more fully in the rest of the Bible. Where appropriate I will relate what is suggested there to later passages.

This universe is God's creation

The first and most obvious truth revealed in the first chapter of Genesis is that this universe and everything in it is God's creation. The words 'created' or 'made' occur 14 times in chapter one and the first four verses of chapter two. This distinction between God and his creation is essential to all biblical thought and to a Christian worldview. It distinguishes Christianity from *monism,* the belief that all reality is ultimately singular — all is One, with no differentiation — a view that is common to Eastern religions. It also distinguishes Christianity from *pantheism*, the belief that God is somehow identical with the totality of the universe — everything is God.

As a created universe, everything is dependent on God for its existence. It is equally true that everything is dependant on its relationship to our creator and redeemer God for its *meaning* and *purpose.* What Paul said of humans in Acts 17:28, '**In him we live and move and have our being,**' could also be said of all creation.

The universe is not divine, nor to be worshipped as such, as in some pagan religions, popular Hinduism and recent New Age borrowings from both. It is true that the Bible sometimes speaks of nature *as a person* (e.g. Leviticus 18:28, Deuteronomy 30:19; 32:1; Psalms 19:1–4; 96:11–13; 98:7–9; Isaiah 1:2). However, these are all figures of speech, *personifying,* not *personalising,* nature. The use of the word 'saw' rather than 'said' in the repeated phrase, '**God saw that it was good**' in Genesis 1, implies a certain separation between God and his creation.

This does not mean that there is not a definite *sacredness* about nature, simply because of its relationship to God. Christopher Wright, in *Old Testament Ethics for the People of God*, summarises this well:

> The Old Testament constantly treats creation *in relation to God*. The created order obeys God, submits to God's commands, reveals God's glory, benefits from God's sustaining and providing, and serves God's purposes — including (but not confined to) the purpose of providing for human beings, or functioning as the vehicle of God's judgment upon them. So there is a sacredness about the non-human created order that we are called upon to honour — as the laws, worship and prophecy of Israel undoubtedly did. But to *worship* nature in any of its manifestations is to exchange the Creator for the created. And that is a form of idolatry against which Israel was repeatedly warned (e.g. Deuteronomy 4:15–20; cf. Job 31:26–28), and which Paul links to the whole tragic litany of humanity's wilful rebellion and social evil (Romans 1:25 and the surrounding context). The radical monotheism of Israel that set itself against all other gods of, or in, nature did not rob nature itself of its God-related sacredness and significance.

As later scriptures explain, God not only brought the universe into being; he is actively sustaining its existence and functions at macro and micro levels. As Elihu rightly said to Job, '**If it were his intention and he withdrew his spirit and breath, all people would perish together and would return to the dust**' (Job 34:14,15; see also Psalm 33:6–9; 36:6; 65:9–13; 104). This world is not a *self*-sustaining biosystem as in some New Age ideas. That is not to say that God has not built into the earth an incredible capacity for renewal, recovery, balance and adaption.

It is significant that Genesis does not state the process by which God made the earth. In my booklet, *The Complementary Nature of Science and Christianity*,* I explore the question of evolution. Here, however, I would point out that there is a hint that God gives to his creation a built-in creative ability of its own. In Genesis 1:11, 20 and 24, the land and the

---

*   This can be read at my website, www.christianity.co.nz

waters are invited to participate in creation by producing vegetation and living creatures, all, of course, under God's direction. Plants and animals are also given the ability to reproduce their own kind. God also invited the fish, birds and humans to *fill* the waters and the earth in imitation of God's own creative acts of filling. Charles Kingsley, in *The Water Babies*, has the mother of creation say: 'Know child, that any one can make things if they take time and trouble enough; but it is not everyone who, like me, can make things make themselves.'

However, the contribution of creatures, which God not only allows, but positively encourages, is clearest and most decisive in the case of humans, created in his image. The fact that there is no conclusion to the seventh day of rest may indicate that, having completed the initial conditions for a meaningful world, at least some of the responsibility now rests with humans. As Henri Blocher comments in *In the Beginning: The opening chapters of Genesis*: 'God's Sabbath, which marks the end of creation, but does not tie God's hands, is therefore coextensive with history.' Richard Middleton adds the suggestive comment:

> God in Genesis 1 is like no one as much as a mother, who gives life to her children, blesses them, enhances their power and agency, and then takes the parental risk of allowing her progeny to take their first steps, to attempt to use their power, to develop toward maturity.

It is also worth noting that the Hebrew *bara*, which is used in the Bible only to refer to God's creation, is used in verse 1 of the creation of matter, verse 21 of the creation of life and three times in verse 27 of the creation of humans. Here we have God's three greatest acts of creation. Though not necessarily meaning to 'create out of nothing', it has the concept of 'initiating something new'. This word is used of God's creative powers 18 times in the book of Isaiah.

There is plenty throughout scripture to indicate that God didn't finish his work with the initial creation, but continues to be active at all levels. This is nowhere plainer than in the Psalms (e.g. 104; 147) passages in Job (e.g. 38:12, 25–27, 41; 39) and in the teaching of Jesus (e.g. Matthew 6:26–30). It is in Christ that '**all things hold together**' (Colossians 1:17).

It is significant also that God's authority over creation provides the foundation for his redemption of his people. This is illustrated in the deliverance of his people from Egypt. Whereas in his acts of creation in Genesis 1, God brings order out of chaos, here he actually *uses* his power over creation for the deliverance from Egypt. This is the central theme of the Song of the Sea in Exodus 15. In Psalm 74 the author appeals to the God whose power split the sea, crushed Leviathan, created the sun and moon, and established the seasons, for his hope of deliverance from the devastating effects of the destruction of Jerusalem and its aftermath. Israel's redemption is to be part of God's new creation.

John Woolman wrote in *Journal*, 'It is not possible to love an unseen God while mistreating God's visible creation.'

What motivates our love of nature? For the Christian, maybe it is because it is not really 'nature' at all. It is God's creation. It bears the stamp of his glory.

God is revealed as the master craftsman

God begins with an earth that is described as '**formless and empty**' (Genesis 1:2) and proceeds to fashion it to sustain life. This is not the 'chaos' of parallel Babylonian creation myths, chaos being the antithesis of 'cosmos'. There is no distortion of God's creation here. It is 'unformed', not 'deformed'. Many texts combine the idea of artisan, with that of God as ruler (e.g. Psalm 119:89–91). The writer of Hebrews tells us that '**the universe was formed at God's command**' ('fashioned by the word of God' — NEB, Hebrews 11:3). The word translated 'formed' is the same word used elsewhere of the potter's activity in making a lump of clay into an earthenware vessel (cf. Romans 9:21). Paul tells us that the nature of God is understood '**from what has been made**' (Romans 1:20 — *ta poiemata*: 'the works of the craftsman's art'). In commenting on the superb literary artistry of the creation story, Middleton, in *The Liberating Image*, says:

> Superimposed on and integrated with the picture of God speaking creation into being is the metaphor of God as designer and artificer, constructing with care, attention, obvious pleasure, and self-investment (as a good artist), a coherent, harmoniously functioning cosmos, according to a well-thought-out plan.

The Hebrew word for 'good' (*tob*), which occurs six times in Genesis 1, has in this context a twofold connotation: aesthetic and ethical. As

Aristotle recognised over two millennia ago, 'In all things of nature there is something of the marvelous.'

Proverbs 14:31 declares, '**Whoever oppresses the poor shows contempt for their maker**' (cf. 17:5). If we are to respect the skill of the one who created humans by the way we treat them, should we not equally respect him who created the universe by similar care of his creation? If a man was to trash something his wife had created with great attention and loving care, what would this say about his regard for her? Maybe we should treat the loss of each species as we would treat the loss of a great work of art, because that is what it is. Calvin DeWitt expresses this most clearly in *Caring for Creation*:

> Jesus Christ is Creator, Integrator, and Reconciler; yet many who call on his name abuse, neglect, and do not give a care about creation. That irony is there for all to see. Honouring the Creator in word, they destroy God's works in deed. Praising God from whom all blessings flow, they diminish and destroy God's creatures here below. The pieces of this puzzle do not fit! One piece says, 'We honour the Great Master!' The other piece says, 'We despise his great masterpieces!'

Contrastingly, we can show our respect for God's creation both by seeking to preserve it, and also in our own creative use of it. Wendell Berry has a significant comment in this respect:

> If we understand that no artist — no maker — can work except by reworking the works of Creation, then we see that by our work we reveal what we think of the works of God. How we take our lives from this world, how we work, what work we do, how well we use the materials we use, and what we do with them after we have used them — all these are questions of the highest and gravest religious significance. In answering them, we practice, or do not practice, our religion.

He is God of all the earth

Genesis 1 also rules out *polytheism*, which was so prevalent in Israel's day. The Bible states that God is '**God over all the kingdoms of the earth**' (2 Kings 19:15), '**God of the whole human race**' (Jeremiah 32:27), '**the God of all the earth**' (Isaiah 54:5), '**the Judge of all the earth**'

(Genesis 18:25), 'the King of all the earth' (Psalm 47:7). 'The Lord is God; besides him there is no other' (Deuteronomy 4:35; cf. 39; see also 1 Samuel 2:2; 1 Kings 8:60; Joel 2:27; Isaiah 45:5,6,18). Referring to the uniqueness of the first commandment, 'You shall have no other gods before me' (Exodus 20:3), Werner Schmidt, in *The Faith of the Old Testament*, comments:

> There is no real model for it, and it cannot be derived from the neighbouring religions, but is opposed to their essential nature. History looks for analogies for all phenomena, but so far as we know at present it is impossible to show that the first and second commandments were borrowed from elsewhere. Exclusiveness of creed is unique to Israel.

James Nash, in *Loving Nature: Ecological integrity and Christian responsibility*, fills out the implications of this in some detail:

> From the perspective of radical monotheism in the doctrine of creation, there are no lesser divinities — not the sun and moon (against the worship of which Genesis 1:14–18 was a reaction), not golden calves and other 'graven images', not sacred groves or ancient trees, not mighty mountains or volcanoes, not fearsome beasts or demons, not caesars or pharaohs or heroes, and not even Gaia or Mother Earth. In this view, polytheism, animism, astrology, totemism, and other forms of nature worship are not only idolatry, but also, as the prophets regularly suggested, vanity and stupidity (cf. Isaiah 40:12–28; 44:9–20; 46:1–11; Acts 14:15). The Creator alone is worthy of worship ... Nevertheless, though only the Creator is worthy of worship, all God's creatures are worthy of moral consideration, as a sign of the worthiness imparted by God and, in fact, as an expression of the worship of God. The monotheistic doctrine of creation does not desacralise nature. Nature is still sacred by virtue of having been created by God, declared to be good, and placed under ultimate divine sovereignty.

The earth belongs to God

By virtue of the fact that he created it, the earth and all that is in it belongs to God. 'To the Lord your God belong the heavens, even the highest heavens, the earth and everything in it' (Deuteronomy 10:14). 'The earth

is the Lord's, and everything in it, the world, and all who live in it;
for he founded it on the seas and established it on the waters' (Psalm
24:1,2; cf. Psalm 50:12).* All that we are and all God has provided for
our wellbeing is provided from his abundant store. In Genesis 1:29, God
gives humankind plants for food. After Noah's flood, God extends this to
'everything that lives and moves' (Genesis 9:3). As Christopher Wright
declares:

> God is the earth's landlord and we are God's tenants. God has
> given the earth into our resident *possession* (Psalm 115:16), but
> we do not hold the title deed of ultimate ownership. So, as in
> any landlord-tenant relationship, God holds us accountable to
> himself for how we treat his property.

We have a responsibility to pass it on in the condition we found it.
Margaret Thatcher got it right when she stated at a Conservative Party
Conference, 'No generation has a freehold on this earth. All we have is a
life tenancy — with a full repairing lease.' Or, in the words of Crocodile
Dundee, humans 'arguing over who owns [land] is like two fleas arguing
about who owns the dog they live on.'

The relationality of God and creation

God exists in relationships of Father, Son and Spirit. Though this is not
spelt out in any detail until we get to the New Testament, there are hints
of it in Genesis 1.** God's spoken word occurs repeatedly in this chapter,
the word which John identifies as the One who 'became flesh and made
his dwelling among us' (John 1:1,14). The 'Spirit of God' is active in
creation, 'hovering over the waters' (Genesis 1:2), bringing order and
fullness out of what was formless and empty. The Hebrew word translated
'hovering' is the same word used in Deuteronomy 32:11 of an eagle
hovering over her young. Father, Son and Spirit are all active in creation.
Many see inklings of the Trinity in the plural 'us' in Genesis 1:26. If God
himself exists in relationships, it is natural to think that this may be true
of his creation.

---

*   See also 1 Chronicles 29:11; Job 41:11.
** For a detailed explanation of biblical teaching on the Trinity, see my booklet,
    Understanding the Trinity, which is available at www.christianity.co.nz

The more we learn about creation, particularly from modern physics, genetics, and biology, the more this is seen to be the case, even in the physical realm. The theory of relativity and quantum physics have revealed the interconnectedness of all creation, and that even matter at the opposite ends of the universe can have a permanent relationship. As Larry Rasmussen put it delightfully in *Earth Community, Earth Ethics*, 'All the createds are related'. Joseph Sittler, in *Gravity and Grace*, likens it to a fine piece of cloth: 'You pull a thread here, and it vibrates throughout the whole fabric.' The eminent naturalist John Muir, in *My First Summer in the Sierra*, said, 'When we try to pick out anything by itself, we find it hitched to everything else in the universe.' The Gaia hypothesis, that the earth and its living creatures form one interconnected system, has positive value for scientific research — though, as Christians, we reject the concept that it is any kind of divine being.

There is plenty of evidence for a certain cooperation between ecosystems in order to produce sustainability and diversity. As Michael Northcott points out:

> Eugene Odum's theory of ecosystems argued for a directedness within all life communities whose goal is the achievement of a stable biomass in any particular system, which can sustain the greatest species diversity. Ecological order is characterised by species diversity, by a stable biomass and by the preservation of nutrients in ecosystems by recycling processes. These processes are reliable and repetitive: they are mostly threatened, not by natural competition or predation, but by humanly originated intervention.

There are ways in which we humans have strong links with the rest of creation. As we shall see, there are significant differences between us and the rest of creation. However, we are all created beings, wholly dependent on God for our existence. It is significant that animals and humans are created on the same day in Genesis 1. As Ken Gnanakan puts it in *Responsible Stewardship of God's Creation*, 'Man did not create the tapestry of life, he is only a thread in it.' We contain clay, minerals and water, and are powered by sunshine through plant life.

On my website, in the booklet *The Complementary Nature of Science and Christianity*, I have given a summary of up-to-date genetic evidence, which I believe is as near as you can get to proof in scientific terms for the fact that humans and the great apes have common ancestry. We share 99 percent of our DNA with them. Biologically we are similar. We eat and reproduce like animals. We breathe the same oxygen molecules breathed by every type of creature ever to have lived on earth. Both animals and humans are described as 'living souls' in both Old and New Testaments (e.g. Genesis 1:21; 2:7; Revelation 16:3 — Hebrew *nephesh*, Greek *psuche*). Humans are not body + soul. When God breathed into the body he had formed from dust (Genesis 2:7), he did not plant a soul within the body. He breathed into the dust and man *became* a living soul. Soul = dust + breath. We are equally mortal with the rest of creatures (1 Timothy 6:15,16). Though the writer of Ecclesiastes was uncertain about a lot of things, he got this one right. '**Surely the fate of human beings is like that of the animals; the same fate awaits them both: As one dies, so dies the other. All have the same breath**' (Ecclesiastes 3:19). It is only through the gospel that one day we may be 'clothed' with immortality (1 Corinthians 15:53,54).

Our link with the rest of creation is powerfully reflected in the statement that God made man (Hebrew: *adam*) out of the '**dust of the earth**' (Genesis 2:7 — Hebrew: *adamah*). No translation catches the richness of the Hebrew pun here. Perhaps a good suggestion would be that God made 'humans out of humus'. 'Humans' and 'humus' have a common derivation, as does the world 'humble'. '**Dust you are and to dust you will return**' (Genesis 3:19). As somebody has said, this is really the story of Dusty and Eve! We are creatures of the earth with feet of clay. The animals and birds were also 'formed out of the ground' using the same words (Genesis 2:19). In Genesis 2 the term for humans (*adam*), whether one regards it as a generic term for humans generally or as a personal name, occurs 18 times. The number of occurrences of words that tell us what humans were either formed from, or where they were placed, are as follows: ground (*adamah*) — five, earth — three, field — three, land — two, garden — five, dust — one. Wendell Berry dislikes the word 'environment' as it puts too much distance between us and where we live. The creation is not something apart from us, the created. It is part of us and we are part of it. Perhaps the best evidence of all that we are unavoidably linked with the rest of creation is given by Paul Hawken:

One quadrillion cells make up a human being, and 90 percent
of them are bacteria, fungi, yeasts, and other microbes, without
which we could not survive. Therein lies the paradox; what
makes us fully human is, well, not human.

In Genesis 9:12,16 and Hosea 2:18 God speaks of his covenant that
encompasses all living creatures in addition to humans. The Hebrew word
here for covenant, *berit*, shares a root with the word *bara*, used in Genesis
to describe divine creativity. This root conveys the sense of binding. God,
humans and all living creatures are bound to each other in a web of
interrelationship.

In Psalm 104:30 we are told that it is the Spirit that creates life and
renews the face of the earth. It is the same Spirit that is operative in our
own lives. He is the Spirit of unity (Ephesians 4:3) who unites us with the
Father, Jesus, and God's people, and provides a link with all creation. In
God in Creation: An ecological doctrine of creation, Jürgen Moltmann says:

> If the Holy Spirit is 'poured out' on the whole creation, then he
> creates the community of all created things with God and with
> each other, making it that fellowship of creation in which all
> created things communicate with one another and with God,
> each in its own way.

However, this is very different from the idea that nature has some kind
of spiritual personality with whom we can merge through meditation
and psychic surrender. That kind of unity is part of pagan religions and
advocated by some New Age gurus, and is also a major emphasis of
Eastern religions. Only humans are created in the image of God. As we
have greater responsibility than the animals, we can also do greater harm.
We are accountable; other creatures are not.

God loves fruitfulness and diversity

This is certainly the impression given from Genesis 1:11–25. It is
sometimes overlooked that the command to be fruitful and increase
in number is given to living creatures as well as humans (Genesis 1:22).
Modern biology and zoology has greatly reinforced this fact. There are
something like 250,000 species of known flowering plants, perhaps
10,000 species of birds, and 30,000 species of epiphytes in the tropics. In

a Peruvian rainforest, Harvard biologist E O Wilson counted 43 species of ant on a single tree. A typical four-mile-square patch of rainforest contains 125 mammal species, 400 bird species, 100 reptile species, 60 amphibian species and 150 butterfly species. It is believed that there may be anything from 5 to 40 million species of living creatures altogether, most still undiscovered. In a thimbleful of earth can be found algae, protozoa, millipedes, beetles, fungi, nematodes, mites, springtails, enchytraeid worms and thousands of species of bacteria — around two billion creatures. It is this biodiversity that provides our own needs for air, light, water, food and shelter. It is unlikely that we could ever provide these needs artificially. 150 of the prescription drugs used in the United States have their origin in plants, fungi or bacteria. Many of these are found in the rainforests. The World Health Organisation estimate that 60 percent of the world's population relies on plants for primary healthcare.

One translation of Genesis 1:20 is, '**Let the waters swarm with swarms of living creatures**.' This was certainly true of the oceans before human intervention and is particularly significant, because the ancient Israelites never got a good look at the underwater world. E O Wilson, who consistently denies the existence of any purposeful order of nature is willing to admit in *The Diversity of Life* that 'the most wonderful mystery of life may well be the means by which it created so much diversity from so little physical matter'. Those of us who believe in the trinitarian nature of the creator, and the kind of relationship that exists between the Father, Son and Spirit, should not be surprised at this. It demonstrates how the deepest community is that which embraces diversity rather than uniformity. Calvin DeWitt reminds us in *Take Good Care: It's God's earth*:

> It is God's will that the *whole of creation* be fruitful, not just
> people. And thus human fruitfulness may *not* be at the expense
> of God's blessing of fruitfulness to other creatures.

From the scientist's perspective, as François Jacob put it, 'Every cell's dream is to become two cells.'

The full value of this diversity has still to be realised by most of us in the Western world, and it is important that we do so before it is too late. The eminent biologist, Sir Ghillean Prance, reporting on South American tribes, says the least efficient tribe utilises 56 percent of all the trees for such products as medicine, clothing, food and shelter. The most efficient uses every last species of tree. In one detailed study, his associates determined that one hectare of tropical forest could yield a net value of US$6820 a year if managed correctly. When the jungle is bulldozed and planted with a single crop, it yields US$3184. If cleared for cattle pasture, as in Brazil, in yields just US$2960.

It is the 'fullness' of the earth that demonstrates God's wisdom and merits praise.

> How many are your works, Lord!
> in wisdom you made them all;
> the earth is full of your creatures.
> There is the sea, vast and spacious,
> teeming with creatures beyond number —
> living things both large and small.
> PSALM 104:24–25

The phrase 'the earth and its fullness' is a characteristic way of talking about the whole environment — sometimes local, sometimes universal (e.g. Deuteronomy 33:16; Psalm 89:12; Isaiah 34:1; Jeremiah 47:2; Ezekiel 30:12; Micah 1:2). Creation not only *declares* the glory of God (Psalm 19:1); creation's fullness is also an *essential part* of it.

And maybe something of this fullness is not limited to this planet. When there was a report of bacteria-like life forms found in a rock from Mars, a newspaper reporter asked Fuller Seminary President Richard Mouw for his reaction. Perhaps he was expecting him to be flummoxed by this development. Mouw simply quoted from the hymn 'How Great Thou Art.' 'O Lord, my God, when I in awesome wonder consider all the worlds thy hands have made!' Scott Hoezee, in *Remember Creation: God's world of wonder and delight*, comments:

> In other words, if there is life on Mars, we Christians will not be
> surprised! It would simply be so typical of God to pepper the rest
> of the universe with creatures even as he has done on this planet.

E O Wilson expresses well the importance of this diversity and the danger of destroying it:

> Biological diversity … is the key to the maintenance of the
> world as we know it. Life in a local site struck down by a passing
> storm springs back quickly because enough diversity still exists.

Opportunistic species evolved for just such an occasion rush in to fill the spaces. They entrain the succession that circles back to something resembling the original state of the environment.

But the restorative power of the fauna and flora of the world as a whole depends on the existence of enough species to play that special role. They too can slide into the red zone of endangered species.

Hildegard of Bingen stated, 'God has made all things in the world in consideration of everything else.' And as Peter Illyn, executive director of Christians for Environmental Stewardship, put it, 'When species go extinct, we're bouncing checks in the trust fund that God called us to manage.'

The goodness of creation

Six times God tells us that what he had made was good and finally that it was 'very good' (vv. 4, 10, 12, 18, 21, 25, 31). The declaration that it is good is made at every stage of creation — from the initial creation of light through to the creation of life on land. This contrasts with early Gnosticism, which taught that the world was an evil place from which people had to be rescued. Gnosticism was a threat to the early church and was fiercely attacked by early Church Fathers such as Irenaeus. Much ancient Greek philosophy tended to downgrade created matter and had an unfortunate influence on some Christian thinking. Such views have lingered in Eastern religions such as Hinduism and Buddhism. Paul reaffirms the goodness of creation in the New Testament in the context of marriage and food: '**For everything God created is good, and nothing is to be rejected if it is received with thanksgiving, because it is consecrated by the word of God and prayer**' (1 Timothy 4:4,5).

This goodness is enhanced by God's blessings on his creation. God blesses the sea creatures and the birds on day five, the humans on day six, and the Sabbath on day seven, when all could rest and enjoy the abundance of creation in relationship with the creator. Christopher Wright expands on this as follows:

> As we read on in Genesis, the creational content of blessings predominates. In fact, the root *brk*, as verb or noun, occurs eighty-eight times in Genesis, which is just over a fifth of all its

occurrences in the whole Old Testament. When God blesses
someone, it normally includes increase of family, flocks, wealth
or all three. God's blessings means enjoying the good gifts of
God's creation in abundance.

And as Hoezee points out, 'It is highly significant that long before
God created human beings in his own image, he gave out his very first
benedictory blessings to our fellow creatures on this planet.'

God's blessings are relational. They concern his protection and
guidance as well as his provision of our needs (e.g. Genesis 48:15,16;
49:24–26). And as Wright explains: 'It is the blessings of God that links
creation and redemption, for redemption is the restoration of the original
blessing inherent in creation.'

The question inevitably arises as to why there is so much apparent
suffering in creation, with so many creatures preying on lesser species. It
has been common in biblical circles to associate this with the Fall, the
rebellion of humans against their creator, imagining that originally all
creatures fed on plants, not other creatures. However, modern knowledge
has made it plain that this was going on millions of years before God
brought humans onto the scene. Others have associated it with an initial
rebellion of Satan in the heavenly realm. But as Christopher Wright states,
in *Old Testament Ethics for the People of God,* 'Predation seems built in
and there is no evidence that it was ever otherwise in the planet's past.'
If it were not so we would certainly have some problems. A lone aphid,
without a partner, breeding unmolested for one year, would produce
enough offspring that if extended in line, they would stretch several
thousand light years into space. It is interesting that ten percent of all the
world's species are parasitic insects. In Psalm 104:27–29 God opens his
hand to satisfy his creatures, but also hides his face and takes away their
breath so that they die and return to the dust, and this seems to be all part
of God's goodness and delight in his creation. I certainly don't profess to
know all the answers to this, but my own view is that the goodness God
describes takes into account the ultimate purpose for which the universe
was made, to reveal the glory of God, and anticipates the time when it
will do so in every detail. I believe this is supported by Paul's statement
in Romans 8:22 that '**the whole creation has been groaning as in the
pains of childbirth right up to the present time.**' The pains of childbirth

are bearable in view of the ultimate purpose and are a necessary part of the process. What may not seem good to us at present will turn out to be good in God's ultimate plans. This is spelt out in some detail by Nash in *Loving Nature*:

> Thus the ecosphere (indeed, the universe) is valued by the Source of value in all its moral ambiguity — including the predation and prodigality that are inherent parts of the dynamics of evolution and ecology, including the inseparable intertwinings of beauty and ugliness, including the combinations of destruction and construction in floods and quakes, including the ordered chaos in the structure of ecosystems, and including the 'purposive randomness' with elements of creative chance structured into generally predictable processes. But God has a mysterious purpose, and God values the creation in its ambiguous state because it contributes to that purpose.

Another important point is expressed by Steven Bouma-Prediger in *For the Beauty of the Earth*:

> Good does not necessarily mean, as many readers assume, perfect. Creation is good but not perfect, at least not (as is commonly understood) in the Platonic sense of perfect as unchanging or static. Though good, the earth still needs to be developed, worked, cared for — the responsibility and the privilege of the human earth-creature.

Loren Wilkinson of Regent College, writer and teacher on environmental issues, makes a relevant point in an article in *Christianity Today*:

> Ecology has been described as the study of who is eating whom, a definition that makes plain that some forms of death are integral to the created order that God called good. Perhaps our repugnance at a biosphere in which creatures eat each other may be a bit like Uzziah's steadying the ark of the covenant. The ark of creation is a rough place, and God's idea of goodness is apparently much wilder than our own.

It is also possible to exaggerate the suffering of creation. Though we must not deny the pain experienced by animals, Charles Raven, theologian and naturalist, makes a relevant point in *Natural Religion and Theology*:

> The cruelty of nature, red in tooth and claw, has been exaggerated. In the absence of a highly developed frontal cortex, the chief ingredients of suffering — memory, imagination and anticipation — may not be there at all. Pain does not take a major part in the experience of any organisms below the human level; and … the life of wild creatures, far from being spent in constant fear is active, rhythmic and, if such a word be allowed, joyous.

Walter Brueggemann, in *Genesis*, says that this goodness is not primarily to be thought of as a moral quality but rather as an aesthetic one. God delighted in how beautiful the creation turned out to be. '[the word good] might better be translated, "lovely, pleasing, beautiful." ' It is easy to gloss over the first part of Genesis 2:9: '**The Lord God made all kinds of trees grow out of the ground — trees that were pleasing to the eye and good for food.**'

The Bible takes the reality of evil very seriously, not as *maya*, an illusion, as in some religious thought. However, in biblical thinking it is an intrusion, whatever and whenever its source, and will have no part in God's ultimate plan.

This goodness of creation is something quite independent of its benefit to or appreciation by humans. It was declared long before humans were around. It has intrinsic goodness, which comes from the God who made it. Walter Harrelson, in a beautiful meditation on Psalm 104:14–15,* notes how the poet's celebration goes far beyond the earth's provision for human needs:

> Storks and goats and badgers do not serve mankind. They do what is appropriate to them, and God provided a place that is itself fulfilling its function when it ministers to the needs of its special creatures. I know of no more direct word from the Bible about the independent significance of things and creatures on which man does not depend for life. The creative and powerful anthropocentrism of biblical religion is here beautifully qualified: God has interest in badgers and wild goats and storks for their own sakes. He has interest in trees and mountains and rock-cairns that simply serve non-human purposes.

---

*   'On God's care for the earth: Psalm 104,' *Currents in Theology and Mission* 2.

On verses 21–26 he observes:

> Man's work is significant, but so is lion's work. Ships doing
> commerce on the high seas are doing significant work, but so is
> Leviathan, trailing behind the ships, blowing and cavorting.

See also Job 38:26,27 where God '**water[s] a land where no one lives, an
uninhabited desert, to satisfy a desolate wasteland and make it sprout
with grass.**'

C S Lewis pointed out that this emphasis, found again and again in
the Bible, of praising God for creatures unconnected to human beings, is
something found almost nowhere else in world literature.

The most positive statement of creation's goodness is that God, in the
person of Jesus, was willing to become part of it, 'Son of Man' (or 'Son of
Adam' — 'son of the soil'). And, as the Bible declares, was willing to die
for it, in order that it might reach its ultimate perfection. In his risen body,
creation has become part of God's nature for eternity.

> Lord God, we praise you for those riches of your creation which
> we shall never see:
> for the stars whose light will never reach the earth;
> for species of living things that were born,
> that flourished and perished
> before mankind appeared in the world;
> for patterns and colour in the flowers,
> which only insect eyes are able to see;
> for strange, high music
> that human ears can never hear:
> Lord God, you see everything that you have made,
> and behold it is
> very good.
>
> DAVID JENKINS, *FURTHER EVERYDAY PRAYERS*

The goodness of creation reveals the goodness of its creator

In other Near Eastern accounts, the powers and gods are portrayed in
various degrees of malevolence. Aspects of the natural order are explained
as the outcome of that malevolence, thus legitimising violence between
humans, and the violent conquest of nature, as it was from violence
between the gods that humans and nature were born. In contrast, in the

Old Testament the goodness of creation is presented as the work of the single good God (e.g. Psalm 19; 29; 50:6; 65; 104; Acts 14:17; 17:26,27; Romans 1:20). Nash has this to say:

> The affirmation of the goodness of creation is also an expression of ultimate confidence in the goodness of God. The world now has an interim goodness. It is not to be despised or rejected or transcended; it is to be appreciated and valued as an expression of the goodness of God. It overflows with marvels and sustains diverse forms of life, for a time. Yet, it is also a world of systematic alienation, in which all life is temporary and destructive of other life. The creation needs liberation and reconciliation. To say with the Nicene Creed that 'all things were made' though Christ is to affirm that the creation as a whole has a redemptive purpose from the beginning. The creation is going on to perfection, ultimately. It is very good because it is being brought to fulfilment by a good God.

Simone Weil once wrote, 'God is good because he delights in the existence of something other than himself.'

God's love for and delight in his creation

It is natural for anyone involved in a creative work, whether artist, engineer or even a child at play, to have some love for and delight in the thing they create. This is surely true of an artist as amazing as God. Though this is not spelt out in Genesis 1, it is clearly stated elsewhere. '**The Lord … has compassion on all he has made**' (Psalm 145:9). Probably the best known verse in the Bible is John 3:16, '**God so loved the world …**'. The Greek word for 'world' is *kosmos*, the natural meaning of which is 'the sum total of everything here and now, *the universe*' as stated in the *Arndt, Gingrich Greek-English Lexicon*. This is in contrast to *oikoumene*, which is merely the world of people. God's care for animals is often mentioned together with his care for humans (e.g. Psalm 36:6; 104; Matthew 10:28–31). The servant God who is '**deeply troubled**' by violence on the earth (Genesis 6:6) and burdened with our sins (Isaiah 43:24) to the extent that he himself was '**crushed for our iniquities**' (Isaiah 53:5), surely includes within that concern the despoiling of his creation, a concern that is such that its renewal is included in the purpose for which Jesus died.

I have no doubt that the reason for the Sabbath rest of Genesis 2:2,3 was to rejoice in all he had made, the same reason for which he has given us the Sabbath. Hoezee speaks of Genesis 1 as a presentation of a 'theology of delight'. Theologian Daniel Migliore writes in *Faith Seeking Understanding: An introduction to Christian theology*:

> We often speak of creation as the work of God. It may be more helpful to think of the creation of the world as the 'play' of God, as a kind of free artistic expression whose origin must be sought ultimately in God's good pleasure.

When God 'laid the earth's foundation ... the morning stars sang together and all the angels shouted for joy' (Job 38:4,7).

God's magnificent description of his creation for Job's benefit, in Job chapters 38 to 41, surely indicates his delight in all he has made. In Job 41:1–5 he teases Job by asking if he can keep crocodiles as pets, as no doubt he does himself. Significantly, he speaks of the hippopotamus as '*first* among the works of God' (Job 40:19, italics mine). I can imagine God's delight in the 'frolic' of whales (Psalm 104:26). This is one of the two places in the Bible where the word 'frolic' appears, the other being Jeremiah 50:11, which speaks of the heifer that frolics as it threshes the grain. The whole of Psalm 104 indicates God's delight in his creation as well as that of the author of the psalm.

As mentioned above, the Hebrew word for 'good' could equally be rendered 'beautiful'. The trees of Eden were 'pleasing to the eye' as well as 'good for food' (Genesis 3:6). There is an African proverb that states, 'When you plant a tree, never plant only one. Plant three — one for shade, one for fruit, one for beauty.' Some of the most dazzling beautiful fish in the word live so deep in the ocean that even if we could get down there we would not be able to see them. But God sees them. 'The Lord does whatever pleases him, in the heavens and on the earth, in the seas and all their depths' (Psalm 135:6). 'May the Lord rejoice in his works' (Psalm 104:31).

When God saved Noah during the flood, he also ensured the continuation of local animal species. When the blood was sprinkled on the Israelite doorposts in Egypt, it was not only the firstborn humans who were spared but the firstborn of their animals also. He spared Nineveh not only for the humans that lived there, but also for the 'many animals' (Jonah 4:11). Jesus did indicate that humans are of more value than sparrows, but that does not mean that sparrows do not have value, as God cares for each of them too. '**Not one of them will fall to the ground outside your Father's care**' (Matthew 10:29). As Christopher Wright says:

> It would be an utter distortion of Scripture to argue that because God cares for us more than for the sparrows, we need not care for sparrows at all or that because we are of greater value than they are, they have no value at all.

James Nash, in *Loving Nature*, sums it up: 'All creatures, human and otherkind, and their habitats, are not only gifts of love but also products of love and recipients of ongoing love.'

God is not unconcerned about those who spoil his creation. The time will come '**for destroying those who destroy the earth**' (Revelation 11:18).

The purpose of creation, the glory of God

The goodness of creation extends to the *purpose* for which God created the universe. Though this is not spelt out it Genesis 1, it is made plain through the rest of scripture. The ultimate purpose is to reveal the goodness and glory of God. Paul tells us that it is God's invisible qualities, specifically '**his eternal power and divine nature**', that '**have been clearly seen, being understood from what has been made, so that people are without excuse**' (Romans 1:20). Old Testament scholar John Stek refers to the cosmos as 'the glory robe of God', a phrase nicely suggested by the opening verses of Psalm 104.

One of the ways in which scripture expresses this ability of nature to reveal God's character is how nature is pictured as worshipping God. '**Let the sea resound, and everything in it, the world, and all who live in it. Let the rivers clap their hands, let the mountains sing together before the Lord, for he comes to judge the earth**' (Psalm 98:8,9; see also Psalm 96:12,13; 145:10,21; 148; 150:6). Psalm 104:31 puts God's glory and God's works of creation in parallel. Psalm 95 invites us to make a joyful noise to God, not only because God is our Saviour but pre-eminently because '**in his hand are the depths of the earth and the mountain peaks belong to him. The sea is his, for he made it, and his hands formed the dry land.**' When the Psalmist begins or ends a Psalm with the phrase '**Praise the Lord**' (e.g. Psalm 148) he is inviting all creation to praise with him. The original Hebrew *hallelu yah* is neither a simple indicative statement nor an exclamatory outburst, but an imperative that invites others to join the chorus of praise to God.

This notion that creation exists for the glory of God is reinforced by the manner in which the Bible appears to speak of creation as God's temple. In Isaiah 66:1,2 God declares, '**Heaven is my throne, and the earth is my footstool. Where is the house you will build for me? Where will my resting place be? Has not my hand made all these things, and so they came into being.**' Thrones and footstools are found in palace-temples. It is as if God is saying, 'Why build a temple when I have already created one for myself — the cosmos?' The Bible also uses metaphors such as foundations, pillars, canopy, windows and storehouses when speaking of the earth. Verbs of building are often used for the act of creation, especially *yasad* and *kun*, which are rendered variously 'to establish, found, secure, make firm' (e.g. Job 38:4–7; Proverbs 3:19,20). Perhaps there is a connection here with the use of 'image' when referring to humans and Jesus. When you build a temple you place an image in it. In this sense, the whole of creation is a sacred place.

Psalm 29 is significant in this regard. The Psalmist describes the power and majesty of the '**Lord**' of glory, '**the God of Glory**', the Lord '**who sits enthroned over the flood**' (vv. 2,3,10) as they are revealed in creation. This world of nature is his '**temple**' in which '**all cry "Glory"**' (v. 9). Hoezee tells of an ornithologist who observed a single red-eyed vireo singing its song 22,197 times in a single day! '**Day after day they pour forth speech**' (Psalm 19:2). Indeed they do, and God is listening. This truth is vividly portrayed in the two great chapters on worship, Revelation 4 and 5. In chapter 4, living creatures surround the throne of God with the faces of a lion, an ox, a man and a flying eagle. Maybe they represent all of creation. '**Day and night they never stop saying: "Holy, holy, holy is the Lord God Almighty who was, and is and is to come"**' (v.8). Surrounding them are the 24 elders, representing the redeemed of the Old and New Covenants. The living creatures, joined by the elders, '**give glory, honour and thanks to him who sits on the throne and who lives for ever and ever**' and say: '**You are worthy, our Lord God, to receive glory and honour and power, for you created all things, and by your will they were created and have their being**' (vv. 9,11). In chapter 5, Jesus appears as '**a Lamb, looking as if it had been slain**' (v. 6). He is then praised by the redeemed for their salvation.

The next circle encompassing the throne is comprised of angels numbering **'thousands upon thousands, and ten thousand times ten thousand'** (v. 11). Especially significant for our purpose is to note that these angels are yet surrounded by another circle comprised of **'every creature in heaven and on earth and under the earth and on the sea, and all that is in them, saying: To him who sits on the throne and to the Lamb be praise and honour and glory and power, for ever and ever!'** (v.13).

Note the following points about this passage:

- The worship begins with who God is in his holy and eternal character.

- Before any mention of redemption, God is worshipped because of his power and glory as revealed in creation.

- All creation, including all living creatures, is involved in this worship. As we shall see, it is the responsibility of humans, as God's priestly representatives, to enhance and give voice to creation's worship.

The Westminster Confession states that, 'Man's chief end is to glorify God and enjoy him forever.' It would be equally biblical to make the same affirmation about the whole of creation. Jürgen Moltmann, in *God in Creation*, says, 'The creatures of the natural world are not there for the sake of human beings. Human beings are there for the sake of the glory of God, which the whole community of creation extols.'

> I think I shall never see
> A poem lovely as a tree:
> A tree that looks at God all day
> And lifts her leafy arms to pray.
>
> JOYCE KILMER

Christopher Wright says:

> We may not be able to explain *how* it is that creation praises its Maker — since we know only the reality of our human personhood 'from the inside', and what it means for *us* to praise him. But just because we cannot articulate the *how* of creation's inarticulate praise or indeed the *how* of God's receiving it, we should not therefore deny *that* creation praises God — since it is affirmed throughout the Bible with overwhelming conviction.

Michael Northcott adds:

> In the Hebrew perspective humanity and the cosmos have moral
> significance, and both are required to make a moral response to
> the creator, a response to God, which reflects his glory and offers
> the return of gratitude, praise and worship.

Bouma-Prediger, in *The Greening of Theology*, says we need to take
seriously this responsiveness of creation. 'All creation is a place of grace.
And all creatures respond to the call of God to be and become, each in
their own creature-specific way.'

Worship and the glory of God are the ultimate purpose of creation.
'**May the whole earth be filled with his glory**' (Psalm 72:19). For those
who have eyes to see '**the whole earth is full of his glory**' (Isaiah 6:3). The
day will come when the earth will be filled with the knowledge of this glory
'**as the waters cover the sea**' (Habakkuk 2:14). How much of the sea is
covered by water? N T Wright has an insightful comment about this verse:

> How can the waters cover the sea? They *are* the sea. It looks
> as though God intends to flood the universe with his love. We
> might even suggest, as part of a Christian aesthetic, that the
> world is beautiful, not just because it hauntingly reminds us of its
> creator, but because it is pointing forwards: it is designed to be
> filled, flooded, drenched in God; as a chalice is beautiful not least
> because of what we know it is designed to contain, or as a violin
> is beautiful not least because we know the music of which it is
> capable.

It is the lack of worship that makes evangelism and discipleship necessary.
John Calvin occasionally pointed out that one of the reasons God created
human beings to stand upright is precisely so we can lift our gaze to the
heavens, praising God for the celestial wonders we see in the night sky.

In view of this purpose of creation, there can be few things that delight
Satan more than to see God's work destroyed. The devil hates nature's
praises. The devil's delight in wrecking creation has been a recurring
theme in literature, such as in John Milton's *Paradise Lost* and the film
version of John Updike's novel, *The Witches of Eastwick*. His dwelling is
pictured as an abode devoid of the beauty found in nature, as in Dante's
Inferno and the land of Mordor in *The Lord of the Rings*.

God's revelation of himself in creation

The Belgic Confession of 1561, in answering the question, 'By what means is God made known to us?', states in its first part:

> By creation, preservation, and government of the universe; which is before our eyes as a most elegant book, wherein all creatures, great and small, are as so many characters leading us to see clearly the invisible things of God.

Genesis 1 enables us to glimpse his extraordinary power, creativity and artistry. The goodness revealed in creation must come from one who is himself the essence of goodness. The beauty seen everywhere in creation is surely designed by One who is himself glorious. Psalm 19 speaks of two ways in which God makes himself known — his created universe and his written word:

> The heavens declare the glory of God:
> the skies proclaim the work of his hands.
> Day after day they pour forth speech;
> night after night they display knowledge.
> They have no speech, they use no words;
> no sound is heard from them.
> Yet their voice goes out into all the earth,
> their words to the ends of the world ...
> The law of the Lord is perfect,
> refreshing the soul.
> The statutes of the Lord are trustworthy,
> making wise the simple.
> The precepts of the Lord are right,
> giving joy to the heart.
> The commands of the Lord are radiant,
> giving light to the eyes.
>
> PSALM 19:1–4,7,8

God's work of creation stirs up our feelings of wonder and praise. God's word, the Bible, makes sense of those feelings.

Larry Rasmussen notes that in the Old Testament redemptive events constantly centre on the creation. God shows up in a bush, in a spring, in an earthquake, on a mountaintop, in the wind (e.g. Exodus 3; 17:1–7; 19:16–19; Job 38:1; 40:6).

Scripture uses nature to teach spiritual truths. God himself used numerous examples from nature to impress Job with his power (Job 38–41). The writings of the prophets contain many illustrations from nature. The Psalms repeatedly use analogies from nature. Jesus constantly illustrated his teaching with lessons from nature. Consider the following aspects of nature that Jesus referred to in illustrating his teaching: lilies, grass, thistles, thorn bushes, mint and rue, wheat, kernels of wheat, mustard seeds, fruit trees, figs, fig trees (dead and living), olive trees and olive oil, mulberry trees, green and dry trees, grapes, wineskins, vines and vineyards, reeds, weeds, manure, bread, flour and dough, birds, sparrows, ravens, vultures, snakes, wolves, foxes, sheep, goats, roosters, worms, puppies, camels, hens and chickens, calves, oxen and donkeys, gnats, moths, flesh and blood, salt, yeast, eggs, millstones, pearls, sea, dust, rust, fire, stones, rocks, sand, storms, rain, heat, famine, earthquakes, pestilences, red sky, clouds, wind, lightning, sun, moon, stars, light and darkness, mountains and hills, springs, running water; and human activities such as shepherding, ploughing, sowing, fishing and milling. He prepared for his ministry by spending 40 days '**with the wild animals**' (Mark 1:13). And Jesus regarded his father's concern for creation as so well accepted that he could build other teaching upon it (Matthew 6:25–34; 10:29–31).

Jesus said we were to '**look at**' the birds of the air (Matthew 6:26). The *Expositor's Greek Testament* gives the emphasis of the Greek here as 'fix your eyes on, so as to take a good look at'. He says we are to '**see**' how the flowers grow. Again, the *Expositor's Greek Testament* gives the emphasis as 'observe well that you may learn thoroughly the lesson they teach'. Jesus would like us to be bird watchers and botanists! Worthy of mentions here is John Stott's delightful book, *The Birds Our Teachers*. Obviously, we have much to learn from nature if only we have eyes to see.

> But ask the animals, and they will teach you,
> or the birds in the sky, and they will tell you;
> or speak to the earth and it will teach you,
> or let the fish of the sea inform you.
>
> JOB 12:7,8

And Peter reminds us that it is scoffers who forget lessons from creation (2 Peter 3:3–7).

Humans have been given the responsibility of *naming* the animals (Genesis 2:19). Naming has a deep personal significance in Hebrew thought. That Adam was called upon to name the creatures implies some knowledge of them so as to get it right. Adam was the first naturalist. It is significant that the first use of human language mentioned in the Bible has to do with our relationship with creation. The second has to do with intimate human relationships (Genesis 2:23).

The book of Proverbs also speaks of the wisdom of God revealed in creation and lessons to be learned from it (e.g. Proverbs 3:19–21; 8:1,22–36; 30:24–28).

St Bonaventure wrote in *The Mind's Road to God*:

> He therefore, who is not illuminated by such great splendour of created things is blind; he who is not awakened by such great clamour is deaf; he who does not praise God because of all these effects is dumb; he who does not note the first principles from such signs is foolish. Open your eyes, therefore, prick up your spiritual ears, open your lips and apply your heart, that you may see our God in all creatures.

I will make rivers flow on barren heights,
  and springs within the valleys.
I will turn the desert into pools of water,
  and the parched ground into springs;
I will put in the desert the cedar
  and the acacia, the myrtle and the olive.
I will set junipers in the wasteland,
  the fir and the cypress together,
so that people may see and know,
  may consider and understand,
 that the hand of the Lord has done this,
  that the Holy One of Israel has created it.
                    ISAIAH 41:18–20

I wonder if it is something of this truth, God revealed in his creation, that Paul has in mind in his puzzling statement to the Colossians: 'This **is the gospel that you heard and that has been proclaimed to every creature under heaven**' (Colossians 1:23). He is very specific concerning the responsibility of those who fail to recognise the revelation of God in creation: '**The wrath of God is being revealed from heaven against** all the godlessness and wickedness of human beings who suppress the truth by their wickedness, since what may be known about God is plain to them, because God has made it plain to them. For since the creation of the world God's invisible qualities — his eternal power and divine nature — have been clearly seen, being understood from what has been made, so that people are without excuse' (Romans 1:18–20). As Philip Sherrard has written in *Human Image: World Image*, 'Creation is nothing less than the manifestation of God's hidden Being.' If we have eyes to see, his fingerprints are everywhere.

Obviously there are some things we cannot learn from nature. But let's be open to what we can. Job had many questions for which he received no answer. However, when confronted with God's description of his creative powers (Job 38–41), the evidence of which surrounded him, and convinced of his goodness, he knew that God was in control and that ultimately things would work out, and with that he was content. He has met God through his creation and has begun to see the bigger picture. No doubt one of the reasons for the incredible vastness of the cosmos is to remind us constantly of who we are in relation to God, lest we should distrust his wisdom or even think we need to know all the answers. As Bill McKibben argues in *The Comforting Whirlwind; God, Job, and the Scale of Creation*:

> God is describing a world without people — a world that existed long before people, and that seems to have its own independent meaning. Most of the action takes place long before the appearance of humans, and on a scale so powerful and vast that we are small indeed in the picture of things.

Maybe we need to ask God to give us the kind of mind expressed by Joseph Sittler in 'Ecological Commitment as Theological Responsibility': 'I have never been able to entertain a God-idea which was not integrally related to the fact of chipmunks, squirrels, hippopotamuses, galaxies, and light years.'

Albert Wolters, in *Creation Regained*, uses a useful analogy of the difference between the revelation of God in creation and that in scripture. Creation is like the blueprint of a building. It can tell us many things about the nature of the creator and give us inklings of his purpose and care for us if we have a heart open to learn. But we have forgotten how to read the blueprint. It is non-verbal. 'They have no speech, they use no words' (Psalm 19:3). We need more specific guidance as to how to read the blueprint. This the Bible provides in much detail. If we are open to all we can learn from both sources, then God can give us the wisdom as to how to make the best use of nature, as Isaiah tells us so expressively (Isaiah 28:23–29).

The beauty and sustaining power of nature is God's gift to us

As we have seen, the creation has independent value apart from its benefit to us, simply because of its value to God himself. However, he has also provided it for our benefit. '**I give you every seed-bearing plant on the face of the whole earth and every tree that has fruit with seed in it. They will be yours for food**' (Genesis 1:29). The permission to eat of *every* tree in the garden comes before the prohibition to eat of one tree (Genesis 2:16,17). God lovingly provides the rains and cycles of water, provides food for creatures, fills people's hearts with joy and satisfies the earth (Psalms 65:5–13; 104:10–18; Acts 14:17). Jesus gave us an example of how to enjoy creation without abusing it. He lived very simply, yet he made gallons of excellent wine at a wedding. He allowed his followers to pick and enjoy food on the Sabbath. He described God's kingdom in terms of food and drink and feasting.

The value of these gifts is beautifully expressed by Sittler:

> Man is not alone in this world, not even when his aloneness is unalleviated by the companionship of his fellowman. The creation is a community of abounding life — from the invisible microbes to the highly visible elephants, the vastness of mountains, the sweep of the seas, the expanse of land. These companions of our creaturehood are not only *there*: they are there as things without which I cannot be at all! They surround, support, nourish, delight, allure, challenge, and talk back to us.*

---

* This responsiveness of creation has been explored by others besides Sittler. For example, in an article in *Cross Currents* 44, no 2 ('Trees, forestry, and the responsiveness of creation'), Brian Walsh, Marianne Karsh, and Nik Ansell claim that both a careful reading of the Bible and a creational listening to the earth lead to the conclusion that trees, for example, have their own peculiar kind of responsiveness.

In ancient Mesopotamia the primary purpose of the cultic system was to obtain divine blessing by providing offerings to the gods. Genesis 1 stands the Mesopotamian worldview on its head. It is God who graciously provides for both humans and animals.

We shall see this more clearly in the chapter on Israel. When we accept the benefits that come to us in nature yet do not recognise the hand of the One who provides them, we act like the Prodigal Son — taking his share of the inheritance and then turning his back on the father who provides it. Encouragingly, this story, in Luke 15, offers a way back.

It is because of the value that his creation holds for God, and his gracious gift of its benefits to us that, Wendell Berry can say, in *Sex, Economy, Freedom and Community*:

> Our destruction of nature is not just bad stewardship, or stupid economics, or a betrayal of family responsibility, it is the most horrid blasphemy. It is flinging God's gifts into His face, as if they were of no worth beyond that assigned to them by our destruction of them.

CHAPTER 7

Humans in God's image

Genesis 1:27 clearly states that humans, as distinct from the rest of the animal creation, have been created in God's image. I have written more fully on the qualities associated with our being created in God's image in the booklet *Who Am I? Finding my true identity as a human being and as a child of God.** My purpose here is to focus only on those characteristics that pertaining to our relationship with God's creation. Being created in the 'likeness' of the triune God, relationships have a very significant part to play in our existence, both with our fellow humans and with the rest of God's creation.

Stewards

Many use the word 'stewardship' to describe our responsibility towards creation. Others have cautioned that the word can convey the mistaken notion that God is an absentee landlord. It is a word that speaks of the management of things, rather than of caring relationships. However, providing we recognise that this is the case, it does carry a clear connotation that we are not the owners of creation, but are accountable to another as to how we manage it. The Greek word for steward in the Bible is *oikonomos*, one who gives order (*nomos*) to a house (*oikos*). 'Eco' derives from *oikos*. The nineteenth-century German biologist Ernst Haeckel coined the term 'ecology' to describe this science of the 'home' we all live in. Whatever else is implied by the term stewardship, it must certainly include sustainable development, which the Au Sable Institute defines as:

---

*   The full text can be read on www.christianity.co.nz

that which seeks to provide an environment that promotes a life of dignity and well-being compatible with the continuation and integrity of supporting ecosystems. The concept includes the concern that material blessings should be available to successive generations as a fundamental God-given right. ('Evangelical Christianity and the environment')

Vice-regents

I like to think of us as God's vice-regents. When the Bible speaks of God's acts of creation and his authority over the earth, it constantly uses the metaphor of kingship. This is clear in several ancient texts (e.g. Exodus 15:18; 19:6; Numbers 23:21; Deuteronomy 33:5) and was common in other Near Eastern cultures long before Israel emerged. It is particularly evident in the Psalms (e.g. Psalm 95:3–5), the Latter Prophets and in Revelation (where the throne of God is mentioned 37 times). The most common term in the Gospels for God's sphere of influence is the 'kingdom of God' or the 'kingdom of heaven'. Jesus used that imagery in several of his parables. Though the word 'king' is not used in Genesis 1 (the first mention of his 'reign' occurs in Exodus 15:18), his absolute authority is obvious. The Hebrew syntax of Genesis 1:26 points to 'rule' as the *purpose*, not simply the consequence or result, of the divine image. It may be that the term 'image' refers to the king's signet ring used to seal wax on documents. In stamping us with his seal he is delegating his authority to us.

A different thought with similar implications, which has been appealed to with increasing frequency, was cited by Gerhard von Rad in *Genesis*:

> Just as powerful earthly kings, to indicate their claim to dominion, erected an image of themselves in the provinces of their empire, where they do not generally appear, so man is placed upon earth in God's image as God's sovereign emblem.

This royal function of the 'image' of God has become a dominant opinion among Old Testament scholars over the last 100 years. It is significant that some ancient Near Eastern texts describe various kings (and sometimes priests) as the image of a god. Edward Curtis, in *Man as the Image of God*, cites texts that designate at least 18 different Egyptian pharaohs as the image of a god. Curtis explains, 'The king as the living image of god was like the cult statue, a place where the god manifested himself and was a primary means by which the deity worked on earth.' It is significant, however, that whereas in the Near East this authority to rule the earth was the responsibility of a few, in Genesis 1 it is delegated to all humans. As Richard Middleton puts it, 'In the Genesis vision, it is ordinary humans (and not some elite class) who are understood to be significant historical actors in the arena of earthly life.' It is also significant that their rule is over the world of nature and not over each other. As Middleton says:

> The democratisation of the imago Dei in Genesis 1 thus
> constitutes an implicit delegitimation of the entire ruling and
> priestly structure of Mesopotamian society (and especially
> the absolute power of the king). The democratisation of the
> image in this text thus suggests an egalitarian conception of the
> exercise of power ... Human beings are called to a fundamental
> mutuality in a shared task, 'a cooperative sharing in dominion,' as
> H D Preuss [*Theological Dictionary of the Old Testament*] puts it.

Jürgen Moltmann, in *God in Creation*, sums it up as follows:

> If it is correct to see the terminology about the image of God as
> derived from royal theology, then this derivation itself contains
> revolutionary political potential: it is not a prince who is the
> image, representative, deputy and reflection of God; it is the
> human being — men and women in like degree, all human
> beings and every human being.

The delegation of this authority to humans is clear in the terms used in Genesis 1:28. We are to '**subdue**' the earth and '**rule over**' its creatures. The Hebrew words are *kabash* and *radah*. These two words both emphasise strongly our right to have dominion over creation in God's scheme of things. *Kabash* comes from a Hebrew root meaning 'to tread down'. This imagery is taken up in Psalm 8:6: '**You made them rulers over the works of your hands; you put everything under their feet.**' Though the word is sometimes used in the context of violent acts of subjugation, of itself it does not have an intrinsically violent meaning. The connotation of *radah* is no less authoritative. The word is often used of the rule of a king or other political leaders in the Old Testament (e.g. 1 Kings 4:24; Psalm 72:8; 110:2). God is clearly setting out in the beginning our dominion over creation, a dominion that is given to no other creatures, not even angels. As Walter Brueggemann puts it, 'There is one way in which God is imaged in the world and only one: humanness!' Psalm 8 explicitly describes this dominion in royal terms. Whereas God is '**majestic**' and his glory is '**above the heavens**', humans, though '**a little lower than the angels**' are '**crowned with glory and honour**' for the purpose of ruling '**over the works of** [God's] **hands**' (vv. 1,5,6). Note that God's name is majestic in *all* the earth (v. 1) and he has put *everything* under the rule of humans (v. 6). Many would see the transforming of culture to God's glory as included in the function of this rule, together with care of the natural realm. According to the worldview of Sumero-Akkadian myths, the gods act in history to change the course of human affairs. So do kings as their representatives on earth. The rest of humans are little more than puppets. However, in the Genesis account, it is ordinary humans who build the first city and are the inventors of metallurgy, music and nomadic livestock breeding (Genesis 4:17,20–22). Ellen Davis, professor of Bible and practical theology at Duke Divinity School, has suggested that instead of *dominion,* we translate the original Hebrew verb in Genesis 1:26,28 as 'exercise skilled mastery'.

God had magnificently filled the '**formless and empty**' planet with living plants and creatures (Genesis 1:20–23) and now calls on humans to complete what he has begun, to build human civilisation and a healthy environment for them to inhabit. As Christopher Wright says, 'To be human is to have a purposeful role in God's creation'.

Albert Wolters, in *Creation Regained: Biblical basics for a Reformational worldview,* suggests an interesting analogy:

> The stage with all its rich variety of props has been set by the stage director, the actors are introduced, and as the curtain rises and the stage director moves backstage, they are given their opening cue. The drama of human history is about to begin, and the first and foundational Word of God to his children is the command to 'fill and subdue'.

In his Dunning Trust Lectures in 1972–3 Ian McHarg traced western man's attitude to the natural world to 'three horrifying lines' in Genesis 1 about the dominion that God gave to humans:

> Dominion is a non-negotiating relationship ... If you want to find one text of compounded horror which will guarantee that the relationship of man to nature can only be destruction, which

will atrophy any creative skill … which will explain all of the
destruction and all of the despoliation accomplished by western
man for at least these 2000 years, then you do not have to look
any further than this ghastly, calamitous text.

However, this is unfair as it ignores both the context of these verses and
the interpretation many Christians have put upon them. As Christopher
Wright points out:

By far the dominant interpretation of these words in both
Jewish and Christian tradition down through the centuries has
been that they entail benevolent care for the rest of creation as
entrusted to human custodianship.

To ignore the context of these verses and what the rest of the Bible has to
say about our attitude to nature, and how this dominion is to be exercised,
is a sure way of misinterpreting scripture. Unfortunately this is a mistake
that many Christians have also made.

In Genesis 2:5 we read, '**The Lord God took the man and put him
in the Garden to Eden to work it and take care of it.**' The word *'abad*,
translated 'work', means 'to serve'. The related noun actually means
'slave' or 'servant'. Though it is the most common Hebrew expression for
agricultural labour, it implies the labour is to be undertaken for the sake of
the earth — not primarily for the sake of the labourer. It implies that the
earth will only bring forth fruit when treated with respect. It is significant
that the word is used in worship (Joshua 22:27) and for the service of the
Levites and priests (Numbers 4:19; 2 Chronicles 8:14). The word *shamar*,
translated 'to take care of', suggests watchful care and preservation. It has
the connotation of 'being vigilant for the sake of another.' The cherubim
placed at the gate were also told to 'keep' or 'guard' it. Cain used the same
word when he asked, 'Am I my brother's keeper?' (Genesis 4:9). Our
dominion is to be exercised in a humble and caring manner. Significantly,
it is the word used in Aaron's benedictory blessing, in which God is
called upon to bless and keep his people (Numbers 6:22–26). It occurs
three times in Psalm 121:7,8 to express God's watchful care of us. Christ,
of course, is our perfect example of what 'keeping' means and how it is
to be exercised. (See John 13:1–17; 17:12). Brian Walsh, in *Subversive
Christianity: Imaging God in a dangerous time*, perceptively points out that
to have dominion is to follow the one we Christians call Domine, Lord,

which means 'to lay down one's life for that which we have dominion over'. We are to '**have the same attitude of mind that Jesus had**' (Philippians 2:5). Or, as Andrew Linzey says in *Animal Theology*, 'the uniqueness of humanity consists in its ability to become the servant species'.

This servant attitude is clearly expressed in Psalm 72:12–14, in which we read of the ideal king:

> For he will deliver the needy who cry out,
>   the afflicted who have no one to help.
> He will take pity on the weak and the needy
>   and save the needy from death.
> He will rescue them from oppression
>   and violence,
>   for precious is their blood in his sight.

Jeremiah 21:11–22:5 holds out these ideals as the criteria by which kingship stands or falls in God's sight. And the Old Testament portrays the arrogance of kings who claim the right of ownership over their resources as if they had created them (e.g. Ezekiel 29:3). As Dave Bookless says, 'Being "under our feet" [Psalm 8:6] is not about trampling down, but symbolic of reflecting God's just and righteous royal authority over creation.'

Loren Wilkinson, in 'The new story of creation: A Trinitarian perspective', an article in *Crux*, says:

> It is our task and nature to understand creation: to name it, to use it — but above all to care for it. And this understanding of a God whose nature is to be in relationship implies a kind of humility and responsiveness in knowing, which has been followed all too seldom in Christendom. N T Wright describes this kind of knowing: 'To know is to be in relation with the known, which means that the "knower" must be open to the possibility of the 'known' being other than had been expected or even desired, and must be prepared to respond accordingly, not merely to observe from a distance.' [*The New Testament and the People of God*].
>
> This kind of knowing, based on relationship and response to the other, should be a corrective to any one-sided understanding of 'dominion.' However we understand the 'dominion' of Genesis 1:28, we can never separate it from the 'keeping' of Gen. 2:15,

which is based on the kind of relational knowledge which Wright describes. We are to 'keep' creation as God 'keeps' us. (The same Hebrew word is used as in the Aaronic Blessing: 'may the Lord bless you and keep you …')

If we are God's vice-regents, then this human dominion must reflect the values and character of God's own kingship. It is significant that the Hebrew word for image, *selem*, in many contexts, refers to a cult image, which in the common theology of the ancient Near East is a localised, visible representation of the divine. In Deuteronomy 10:14–19, God's *reign* is put alongside his *justice* and *compassion*. The writer of Psalm 89 declares: **'Righteousness and justice are the foundation of your throne; love and faithfulness go before you'** (v. 14). Similarly, Psalm 145 expresses well God's attitude. The writer, who speaks of God as **'my God the King'** (v. 1), praises him for his power, compassion, love, goodness, faithfulness and righteousness in relation, not only to humans, but to **'all he has made'** (vv. 7–9,13–17). Robert Murray, in *The Cosmic Covenant: Biblical themes of justice, peace and the integrity of creation*, comments:

> These are, of course, royal qualities; without using the word, the author of Genesis 1 celebrates the Creator as *King*, supreme in all the qualities which belong to the ideal of kingship; just as truly as Psalms 93 and 95–100 celebrate the divine King as Creator.

A king exists for the benefit of his people, not vice versa. The metaphor that expresses this, and which was common as a metaphor for kingly rule throughout the ancient Near East and not just in Israel, was that of the shepherd. Ezekiel gives a superb description of what true kingly shepherding ought to look like in chapter 34.

I have outlined above what the Bible has to say about God's delight in and care for his creation. If we were intended to express God's likeness, however much that likeness may be distorted by our human rebellion, then we should express similar delight and care. To be holy, because God is holy, is the command of both testaments (Leviticus 19:2; 20:26; 1 Peter 1:15,16; cf. Ephesians 5:1). Wendell Berry has this to say:

> In the Bible we find none of the industrialist's contempt or hatred of nature. We find, instead, a poetry of awe and reverence and profound cherishing, as in these verses from Moses' valedictory blessing of the twelve tribes:

> About Joseph he said:
> 'May the Lord bless his land with the precious dew
>   from heaven above
>   and with the deep waters that lie below;
> with the best the sun brings forth
>   and the finest the moon can yield;
> with the choicest gifts of the ancient mountain
>   and the fruitfulness of the everlasting hills:
> with the best gifts of the earth and its fullness
>   and the favour of him who dwelt in the burning bush.'
>   DEUTERONOMY 33:13–16

Berry says, 'Good work honours God's work. Good work uses no thing without respect, both for what it is in itself and for its origin.' And as Carolyn Arends puts it in an article in *Christianity Today*, 'When we make something — when we participate in bringing "cosmos out of chaos," as writer Madeline L'Engle puts it — we affirm the fact that we are made in the image of the Creator.' Any violence is the result of the Fall (Genesis 6:11), a misuse of the authority granted in the original mandate.

Care of creation is a joint activity between God and humans. Miroslav Volf, in *Free of Charge: Giving and forgiving in a culture stripped of grace*, points out that both are necessary for providing a suitable habitat for humans on earth. In Genesis 2:5 we are told there were two reasons that 'no shrub had appeared on the earth and no plant had yet sprung up'. The first was because 'the Lord God had not sent rain on the earth'. The second was because 'there was no one to work the ground'. Volf comments:

> The simple story makes a profound point: For creation to exist as a habitat for humanity, both God and human beings have to do their parts. Human beings cooperate with God in the work of creation.

Psalm 147 illustrates well this principle, speaking both of God's direct activity in creation and his indirect activity through the giving of his laws that point to our responsibilities (vv. 15–20).

Priests

Another biblical picture others see concerning our responsibilities as humans created in God's image is that of priest. In the ancient Near East, royal and priestly functions concerning the mediation of the divine tended to converge. The fact that all humans share the image of God suggests that humans do not need the mediation of God's presence by either kings or priests. Here we see the foundation of the later Christian belief of the 'priesthood of the believer'. Only when humans treat the earth as a gift, and offer the fruits of the earth to God in true worship, can they achieve a right relation with the created order. As we shall see, Israel was called to play a priestly role in mediating God's nature and qualities to all the nations (Genesis 12:3; Exodus 19:6). This role is now the responsibility of all God's redeemed people in whom he is seeking to restore his image. '**You have made them to be a kingdom and priests to serve our God, and they will reign on the earth**' (Revelation 5:10; cf. 1 Peter 2:9). It is the role of priests to represent the interests of the creator in his world, in a witnessing and teaching role (Isaiah 43:12; Luke 24:48; Acts 1:8), and also to bring the needs and concerns of the world before their creator in worship.

Commenting on Romans 8 ('**We know that the whole creation has been groaning as in the pains of childbirth right up to the present time**' 8:22), Charles Cranfield suggests that the universe is unable to do its part in praise to God unless humans do their part. Stones and trees and cats are not as articulate as we are. We can put into words the grateful praises that they would express if they could. Dave Bookless suggests the image of a conductor who enables each instrument of the orchestra to play its part in harmony. Jürgen Moltmann, in *God in Creation*, writes, 'in praise of creation the human being sings the cosmic liturgy, and through him the cosmos sings before its Creator the eternal song of creation.' According to Orthodox writer Philip Sherrard, in *Rape of Man and Nature*, modern science has obscured the essential orientation of humanity towards the transcendent God, and the scientist has taken the place of the priest, bringing to birth a new kind of society oriented towards consumerism rather than the eucharistic worship of God.

Christopher Wright sums up this joint picture of kings and priests as follows:

> Greg Beale argues persuasively [in *Temple and Church's Mission*] that there are theological connections between the tabernacle/ temple in the Old Testament and (1) the picture of Eden in the creation narrative, and (2) the picture of the whole cosmos

restored through Christ to be the dwelling place of God. The temple is a microcosm, both of the primal creation reality and of the new creation reality. In both cases we see God dwelling in the earth as his temple, with human beings serving him and it as his appointed priesthood.

The dual account of the mandate God gave to humanity in Genesis 1–2 uses the language of both kingship and priesthood. Humanity is to rule over the rest of creation, and Adam is put in the garden in Eden 'to work it and take care of it.' Ruling is the function of kingship; serving and keeping were major functions of priests in relation to the tabernacle and temple.

CS Lewis, who wrestled in many essays with the senselessness of animal suffering, argued that it was precisely because humans are higher than animals in creation's hierarchy that they should oppose animal cruelty. Our superiority to animals ought to motivate us 'to prove ourselves better than the beasts precisely by the fact of acknowledging duties to them which they do not acknowledge to us.'

It is true that this image of God in humans has been defaced by our disobedience. However, the whole purpose of salvation is to renew this image. Brian Walsh and Sylvia Keesmaat, in *Colossians Remixed: Subverting the empire*, have this to say:

> Remember also that Paul says the new community 'is being renewed in knowledge according to the image of its creator' (Colossians 3:10). The clear allusion to the opening chapters of Genesis raises the question for us of how this renewed image-bearing community tills and cares for the rest of creation. If we are renewed in the image of the Creator, then we must ask how the virtues of such renewal transform and reshape our stewardship of the earth.

Christ, of course, in his humanity, is the perfect example of what that image should be (Colossians 1:15), to which he is now seeking to restore us (2 Corinthians 3:18). It is significant that in 2 Corinthians 4:4 the glory of Christ is linked directly with this image. When Paul speaks of Christ as the image of God in Colossians 1:15, he immediately links it with the creation of the universe.

CHAPTER 8

The spoilt image and its effect on creation

Chapter 3 of Genesis describes the disobedience of humans to their creator and hints at its effect on the natural world. This Christian doctrine of the Fall of men and women from their original position of intimacy with their creator is the most reasonable explanation provided by any philosophy or religion, for both the dignity and the degradation of humans; how it is that they can rise to such inspiring heights of moral and creative goodness and yet fall to such depths of evil. Bertrand Russell suggested that original sin was the one Christian doctrine for which there is empirical evidence. The consequence of the Fall was that, as humans 'increased' on the earth (Genesis 6:1 — the verb *raba*), wickedness also became 'great' (Genesis 6:1 — *rab*). One thing that is clear from the Bible is that there is a very definite link between human disobedience to God and the health of the natural order.

There is one aspect of this subject over which Christians disagree that is directly related to one's belief concerning the age of the earth. Are death and other seeming imperfections in nature the result of human sin, or are they part of God's original creation before the advent of humans? In my booklet, *The Complementary Nature of Science and Christianity,* I have given my personal views on this, so I won't deal with it here.* Here let us focus on those matters the Bible is clear about.

Genesis 3:17 indicates the definite connection between human behaviour and the natural environment. '**Cursed is the ground** *because*

---

* This can be read at www.christianity.co.nz

of you' (italics mine). The following verses imply that it will only be by burdensome labour and constant vigilance that humans will be able to provide for their personal needs. As we explore the rest of the Bible we find that there are two ways in which nature is affected by the sins of humans: firstly, by their own destructive actions, and secondly, by behaviour that results in God's judgements, in which he uses natural causes to execute his purposes.

The first of these is obvious enough. Bishop Fulton Sheen, in *Those Mysterious Priests*, says, 'Ecological garbage is only the outward sign of moral garbage piled up in the hearts of men.' Such things as false worldviews, religions that devalue God's creation, wilful ignorance, injustice and plain old self-centredness all have their effect in degrading our natural environment.

The second point may not be proved from mere observation, but it is spelt out time and again in scripture. Judgements sent by God on humans but which have their effect on the natural environment occur often in the Bible. In fact, it is often by causing upsets in their environment that God shows his displeasure of human behaviour. In the book of Genesis we have the curse on the ground recorded in 3:17,18. The flood of Noah's day caused much environmental destruction (chapter 7). The destruction of Sodom and Gomorrah was a major environmental catastrophe (chapter 19). The seven-year famine in Egypt that brought Joseph to power was foretold by God and used for his purposes, though in this instance we are not specifically told that this was the result of judgement (chapter 41).

In the laws given through Moses at Mount Sinai and repeated on the plains of Moab there were severe warnings that if the Israelites were to refuse to listen to God and keep his commands then they would experience drought, attacks from wild animals and plagues, among other catastrophes (Leviticus 26; Deuteronomy 28). If they indulged in idolatry and immorality, the land would be defiled and vomit out its inhabitants (Leviticus 18:24–28). Conversely, if they remained faithful to him, he would assure them of many blessings resulting from the productivity of their environment (e.g. Deuteronomy 28:1–6).

When we come to the prophets we find a similar emphasis. Hosea relates environmental degradation to the wickedness of the people:

There is no faithfulness, no love,
  no acknowledgement of God in the land.
There is only cursing, lying and murder;
  stealing and adultery;
They break all bounds,
  and bloodshed follows bloodshed.
Because of this the land dries up,
  and all who live in it waste away;
The beasts of the field, the birds in the sky
  and the fish in the sea are swept away.

HOSEA 4:1–3

Joel describes a devastating plague of locusts that could only be averted by the repentance of the people (Joel 1, 2). Amos lists the environmental judgements God had inflicted on his people in hope of bringing them to a better frame of mind (Amos 4:6–12). As the exile of God's people to Babylon approached, at the beginning of the sixth century BC, Jeremiah warned that not only would the people suffer, but that the natural environment would be devastated as a result of their evil (e.g. Jeremiah 3:1–5; 4:23–28; 5:24; 12:4; see also Isaiah 5:9,10; 24:1–6; Zephaniah 1:1–6). Much of this destruction would be caused by the invading armies but it was the Lord who had sent them (e.g. Jeremiah 12:10–13). The Old Testament prophets saw ecological damage as the result of exploitation of the poor, rejection of God's covenant and the neglect of true worship.

However we understand the seal and bowl judgements of the book of Revelation (chapters 6 and 16), it is clear that God's judgements have severe environmental consequences.

It is significant that in the one instance that the Bible refers to the 'healing of the land' (2 Chronicles 7:14), it comes about by repentance and returning to God — not primarily by downsizing, recycling, or resource management. Some extraordinary stories have arisen around the world when communities have turned to God in repentant prayer and obedience. One of the most remarkable has been reported from Alemolonga, in Guatemala, where almost sterile land has been transformed into fertile fields yielding huge vegetables as a local community has turned from crime and immorality to Christ.

The Bible tells us in the above instances that destruction of the environment may result from the judgement of God or the direct action of human beings. However, it is our faulty behaviour, resulting from our rebellion against God, which is the ultimate cause. Without having the inspired insight of the prophets of old we would be unwise to be dogmatic concerning the cause of some of our modern catastrophes. As regards those caused by global warning, I would side with those that put at least some of it down to the thoughtless behaviour of human beings. However, if God acted in direct judgement on his people in the past I see no reason to suppose he would not do so today.

Richard Bauckham, in 'First steps to a theology of nature', *Evangelical Quarterly* 58, expresses well the inevitable effects of sin on the environment:

> How does the Fall affect nature? Is it only in human history that God's creative work is disrupted, necessitating a redemptive work, whereas in the rest of nature creation continues unaffected by the Fall? This cannot be the case, because humanity is part of the interdependent whole of nature, so that disruption in human history must disrupt nature, and since humanity is the dominant species on earth human sin is bound to have very widespread effects on nature as a whole. The Fall disturbed humanity's harmonious relationship with nature, alienating us from nature, so that we now experience nature as hostile, and introducing elements of struggle and violence into our relationship with nature (Genesis 3:15,17–19; 9:2).

This does not necessarily mean that human sin is responsible for all the phenomena in nature that are threatening to humans (earthquakes, floods, volcanoes, tsunamis, etc.), or morally disturbing (the preying of life forms on one another), but it does mean that the Fall distorted our relationship with the earth and frustrated creation's primary function in relation to God.

As we shall see when we come to the New Testament, Christ is the perfect image of God (Colossians 1:15), the second and last Adam (1 Corinthians 15:45–47). As such, through his death, resurrection and exaltation to the throne of God, he has defeated Satan, the 'prince of this world' (John 14:30), and reclaimed for humanity the original purpose: to rule the world on God's behalf.

CHAPTER 9

God's covenant with Noah

G od's concern for the world of nature is a significant part of the story of Noah and the flood in Genesis 6–9. Though living creatures were included in the judgement that came upon humans, God is at pains to ensure the survival of the species. To achieve this he called upon a faithful human to help him, as he still does. Here we have the first Endangered Species Act — initiated by God and carried out by Noah. God does not ask him to preserve the species just because they are of value to Noah for food or as pets or whatever, but '**to keep their various kinds alive throughout the earth**' (Genesis 7:3). These creatures matter because they matter to God. Rabbinic commentators suggest that this careful attention to animals and other creatures was a key lesson of the Noah story. It is as if God has Noah build the ark to train him in caring for creation. To care for creation was the first purposive statement made about the human species in Genesis 2. The covenant with Noah effectively renews this mission, within the context of God's own commitment to creation. We could compare this story with that of the deliverance from Egypt, where the blood on the doorposts was to cover the firstborn of animals as well as the firstborn of humans (Exodus 12:12,13).

Noah's first act after leaving the ark was to offer sacrifices to the Lord. Michael Northcott's comment on this is relevant:

> This primordial sacrifice attempts to restore the fallen creation and to bring it back from its path toward destruction, on which the flood is seen as the judgment of God. Noah recovers what others in his generation had lost, which is humanity's priestly vocation to offer up, from the abundant gifts of creation,

sacrifices which atone for sin, which are pleasing to the Creator,
and in which creation is restored to the order which is the work
of its maker.

The superiority of humans, created in God's image (Genesis 9:6), is
clearly indicated in this story. Noah is given permission to eat flesh as
well as plants. However, there is one proscription. Humans are not to
eat meat with the lifeblood still in it as a sign of respect for the origin of
all life in the divine creation. Later instructions indicate that it must be
returned to the earth (Deuteronomy 12:23,24). The Hebrew word for
'life' in Deuteronomy 12:23 is *nephesh,* which means breath. This reflects
the breath of the creator Spirit. Medical science has shown the intimate
connection between the act of breathing and blood.

After the flood, when God makes a covenant with Noah, all living
creatures, and the earth itself, are included. To emphasise this, it is
repeated six times in the story. '**I now establish my** *covenant* **with you
and with your descendants after you and with every living creature that
was with you — the birds, the livestock and all the wild animals ... every
living creature on earth ... This is the sign of the** *covenant* **I am making
between me and you and every living creature with you a** *covenant* **for
all generations to come ... I have set my rainbow in the clouds, and
it will be a sign of the** *covenant* **between me and the earth ... I will
remember my** *covenant* **between me and you and all living creatures
of every kind ... I will see it and remember the everlasting** *covenant*
**between God and all living creatures of every kind on the earth ... This
is the sign of the** *covenant* **I have established between me and all life
on the earth**' (Genesis 9:8–17, italics mine). Brian Walsh and Sylvia
Keesmaat comment:

> Because all of creation is party to the covenant, it is not
> surprising that stones can bear witness to covenant ceremonies
> (Joshua 24:27), donkeys can speak the word of the Lord
> (Numbers 22:22–30), the land can grieve and vomit out its
> inhabitants (Leviticus 18:28; Jeremiah 4:23–28; 14:2–6; Romans
> 8:22,23), trees and hills can sing for joy (Psalm 96:12; 98:8),
> mountains can hear words of prophecy directed only to them
> (Ezekiel 36:1–15), and even roadside rocks recognize their
> Redeemer (Luke 19:40).

Jeremiah has a similar inclusive emphasis in chapter 33 where he compares God's covenant with David with his faithfulness to day and night and to heaven and earth (vv. 20,21,25,26). As Michael Northcott suggests, it is significant that in his covenant with Noah God does not repeat the commands to subdue and have dominion. Having mistaken dominion for domination, humans had perverted their royal responsibility and polluted the earth. This covenant is both an '**everlasting covenant**' (Genesis 9:16) and unconditional. The sign given that God will be true to his word is the rainbow, the sign of mercy that appears between us and the storm clouds of judgement. It has been suggested that this bow is the bow and arrow, aimed at the heart of God lest he forget his covenant promise.

CHAPTER 10

Lessons from Israel

The first two chapters of Genesis tell us of the creation of the universe
and God's vision for his extended family of humans, created in his own
image, whom he has appointed as his vice-regents to care for the planet in
which he delights so much. However, over the next nine chapters it looks
as if this vision has, bluntly, turned to custard. We read of murder (4:8)
and its glorification (4:23,24), violence that had reached such an extent
that God felt he had to have a fresh start (6–9), the misuse of God's gifts
(9:20,21) and attempts to build civilisation by human effort apart from
God (10). However, God is not prepared to give up on his grand design
(which, according to modern science, he had been working on for over
thirteen billion years). His rescue plan, somewhat surprisingly, is to start
with one man, Abraham.

The call of Abraham in Genesis 12 is the beginning of the story of
Israel, and in this call we catch a glimpse of the scope of God's plan for the
saving of mankind and the renewal of creation. '**I will make you into a
great nation, and I will bless you; I will make your name great, and you
will be a blessing. I will bless those who bless you, and whoever curses
you I will curse; and all peoples on earth will be blessed through you**'
(Genesis 12:2,3). As Abraham travels to the land of Canaan in obedience
to God's command, he is given an additional promise: '**To your offspring
I will give this land**' (Genesis 12:7). Later still comes the promise:
'**Through your offspring all nations on earth will be blessed, because you
have obeyed me**' (Genesis 22:18).

So the story goes something like this: God's plan was to build a people
loyal to himself who would inherit the land of Canaan, a people whose

values, laws, and style of living would be an example to the nations (Deuteronomy 4:5–8) and through whom eventually all the nations of the earth would be blessed. This people came to be known as Israel, named after Abraham's grandson. This thought, that it was God's intention to bless all the nations through Abraham and his descendants, is pivotal in the book of Genesis. So important is it that it occurs five times, with minor variations of phraseology (12:3, 18:18; 22:18; 26:4,5; 28:14).

This emphasis is particularly prominent in the Psalms. George Peters, in *A Biblical Theology of Missions*, counts

> more than 175 references for a universalistic note relating to the nations of the world. Many of them bring hope of salvation to the nations ... Indeed, the Psalter is one of the greatest missionary books in the world, though seldom seen from that point of view.

Isaiah spells out clearly God's ultimate intention: '**In days to come Jacob will take root, Israel will bud and blossom and fill the world with fruit**' (27:6). Though these blessings would ultimately come through God's personal intervention in the coming of Jesus (as Paul explains in Romans 15:8,9), their example was intended to light the way for others and so prepare for his coming. In fact, it could be said that all God's dealings with Israel throughout the Old Testament period were that he might be known throughout the earth.* Only as people acknowledge their true God could they be blessed as he intended.** Psalm 67 spells this out clearly. The reason the psalmist desires God's face to shine on them is that '**[his] ways may be known on earth, [his] salvation among all nations**' (Psalm 67:1,2) and that God may bless his people '**so that all the ends of the earth will fear him**' (v. 7).

In Exodus 19:5 God describes Israel as his '**treasured possession**'. The Hebrew word is *segulla*, which was used in both Hebrew and Akkadian to describe the personal treasure of the monarch and his family

---

*   E.g. Joshua 2:11; 4:24; 1 Samuel 17:46; 2 Samuel 7:23,26; 1 Kings 8:41–43,60; 2 Kings 19:19; Nehemiah 9:10; Psalm 106:8; Isaiah 37:20; 45:6; 63:12; Jeremiah 32:20; 33:9; Ezekiel 36:23; Daniel 9:15.

** The Old Testament scriptures look forward to the time when the nations would not only be *joined* to Israel, but actually be *identified as* Israel, with the same names, privileges and responsibilities before God (Psalm 47:9; Isaiah 19:19–25; 56:2–8; 66:19–21; Amos 9:11,12; Zechariah 2:10,11). For New Testament fulfilment see Acts 15:16–18; Ephesians 2:11–3:6.

(cf. 1 Chronicles 29:3; Ecclesiastes 2:8). God chose to place Israel in a special personal relationship within his worldwide kingship. What this involves is explained in verse 6. Their role is to be a priestly and holy community in the midst of the nations.

As the story progresses, we read how time and again Israel failed to measure up to their God-given task, eventually reaching the point at which God allowed them to suffer the ignominy of the destruction of their land and 70 years captivity in Babylon. However, God was not to be thwarted. Though the nation as a whole was not up to the task, there were still individuals who were faithful to the original vision and who longed for its fulfilment. It was through these that God was able to continue his plans and prepare his people for the final act of the drama.

The Hebrew word 'offspring' in Genesis 12:7 is literally 'seed' and may be either single or plural. As Paul explains in Galatians 3, God's ultimate plan would be fulfilled though a single individual who himself would take over the mission originally given to Israel. This individual, foretold by many of the Old Testament prophets, would succeed where others had failed. It is this person, Jesus (the Second Person of the Divine Trinity of Father, Son and Spirit), born of an Israelite virgin, and his committed followers (the true children of Abraham as per Galatians 3:7), to whom is now committed the original charge of bringing God's blessings to all the nations of the earth. As James pointed out to the leaders of the church in Jerusalem, the bringing of the Gospel to the Gentiles was consistent with the teaching of Israel's prophets, who foretold that they would be welcomed into the divine presence in the temple of messianic age (Acts 15:13–18; see Amos 9:11,12*).

If Israel was to have such a significant role in God's purpose for bringing blessing to the nations, it is most important that we are clear about the kind of people they were intended to be. Though their culture and environment would be very different to many nations in today's world, there are basic principles exemplified in the laws that God gave them that are applicable to all people of all ages. These laws, given through his faithful servant Moses at Mount Sinai, and repeated is some detail as they were about to enter the promised land 40 years later, give

---

* See also Psalm 96:7,8; Isaiah 2:2,3; 25; 56:6,7; Jeremiah 3:17; Micah 4:1,2; Zechariah 14:16).

us the blueprint of a nation that I am sure most of us would indeed find a blessing if they were adhered to. So let's see what we can learn from the kind of nation God intended them to be.

An emphasis on land

It is significant that the covenant promise to Abraham that launched the work of redemption in history included land as a fundamental constitution of that promise. Out of 46 references to the promise from Genesis to Judges, only seven do not mention the land, while 29 are mainly or exclusively about it. In Genesis 28:4 the 'blessing given to Abraham' simply means possession of the land. The Old Testament refers to land 2000 times and the New Testament 250. In his important book, *The Land*, Walter Brueggemann argues that 'Land is a central, if not the central theme of biblical faith.'

This particular land was a wonderful gift to Israel. It was 'a good land — a land with streams and pools of water, with springs flowing in the valley and hills; a land with wheat and barley, vines and fig trees, pomegranates, olive oil and honey; a land where bread will not be scarce and you will lack nothing; a land where the rocks are iron and you can dig copper out of the hills' and 'a land of mountains and valleys that drinks rain from heaven' (Deuteronomy 8:7–9; 11:11). It was indeed, as they were often reminded, a 'land flowing with milk and honey' (e.g. Numbers 13:27). In a wide variety of contexts in the ancient world 'milk and honey' were the food of the gods. As Nobert Lohfink says in *Option for the Poor*: 'What we have here, then, is an image of the plenitude of paradise.'

However, possession of the land and its blessings was not without conditions. Specific instructions were given as to how the people were to treat it, live in it and honour the one who had gifted it to them. On a number of occasions they were warned that if they were not faithful to him and did not observe his laws, then they would forfeit this right and be taken from it (e.g. Deuteronomy 4:1–40; 28:63,64). Gratitude towards the One who had given them the land would prove the best antidote to pride and to neglect of the commands relating to its care (Deuteronomy 8:10–20). If they continued to obey his commands, then not only would he grant many material blessings, but he would 'walk among' them

(Leviticus 26:12, using the same unusual form of the verb as is used to describe God walking with the couple in the Garden of Eden). A further result would be that '**All the peoples of the earth will see that you are called by the name of the Lord**' (Deuteronomy 28:10). The possession of the land was the assurance that they were the Lord's people as promised to Abraham. It is striking that the name of their ancestor Israel came to denote both the people and the land.

Ownership of the land

The divine ownership of the land had been hinted at in one of the earliest pieces of Israelite poetry, the song of Moses and Miriam in Exodus 15, which they sang on their deliverance from the army of Pharaoh. It looks forward to entry into the promised land, which is described as '**your holy dwelling**' (v. 13), '**the mountain of your inheritance**' (v. 17) and '**the place, O Lord, you made for your dwelling**' (v. 17). This theme is found often in the prophets and Psalms. The clearest statement, however, is given in the instructions concerning the Year of Jubilee given to Moses on Mount Sinai. '**The land must not be sold permanently, because the land is mine and you reside in my land as foreigners and strangers**' (Leviticus 25:23; cf. 2 Samuel 20:19; 21:3; Jeremiah 2:7; 16:18). Christopher Wright translates this, 'you are "guests" and "residents" with me.' That the land and its blessings were gifts of grace from God in view of his covenant promises to their forefathers, and not due to their own merit, was emphasised (Deuteronomy 7:7–9; 8:17,18). Should they fail to honour this, they would perish from it (Deuteronomy 4:25,26).

The people of Israel were given the right to private ownership of the land, but only as tenants. And, as we shall see, ownership of the land involved responsibilities: to God, to one's family and to one's neighbours. In the Canaanite system kings owned the land of the small city-states they ruled. Fairness and justice therefore depended on the character of the king. Under the Israelite system God was the ultimate title owner. Fairness and justice were therefore guaranteed as long as they remained faithful to him.

In addition, the land was divided in such a way as to give each individual family a fair share of its resources. First of all it was apportioned fairly to each of the tribes according to the population of that tribe (Numbers 26:52–56). Then, within the tribal boundaries, it was divided 'according to its clans', the constant repetition of this phrase in Joshua indicating that the land should be distributed throughout the whole kinship system as widely as possible. This did not mean that everyone should have the *same*, but that each family should have *enough*. These smaller portions also were held as a gift from God (e.g. Deuteronomy 26:10). In this way, each individual household could claim that the Lord himself guaranteed its right to the land it possessed. This would explain Naboth's resistance to King Ahab's attempts to buy his vineyard (1 Kings 21). 'The Lord forbid that I should give you the inheritance of my fathers' (1 Kings 21:3). The Lord did forbid it. Only by falsely charging Naboth with blasphemy could Ahab appear to give some legitimacy to his theft. As possession of the land was a significant part of the covenant relationship with God, forfeiting his right to membership of the people of God through blasphemy, also forfeited his right to possession of the land. This emphasis on continued ownership of the land discouraged mass migration to cities, so Israel experienced no large-scale urbanisation. It also restricted the development of a class-based social structure.

To ensure that this right to possession of their family inheritance was maintained, every 50 years the year of Jubilee was to be proclaimed. Not only were bonded workers to be freed on this day, but also, if for any reason they had forfeited their land, it was to be returned to them (Leviticus 25:9,10). It is significant that the Jubilee was to be proclaimed on the Day of Atonement. The day on which the people's need for God's forgiveness was acknowledged and celebrated was the day on which forgiveness was to be extended to others.

Failure to observe this right of each to their own inheritance was one of the sins denounced most strongly by the prophets.

> **Woe to those who plan iniquity**
>   **to those who plot evil on their beds ...**
> **They covet fields and seize them,**
>   **and houses, and take them.**
> **They defraud people of their homes,**
>   **they rob them of their inheritance.**
>   MICAH 2:1,2

Woe to you who add house to house
  and join field to field
till no space is left
  and you live alone in the land.

ISAIAH 5:8

No tribal land was to be sold to another tribe, so each Israelite could retain the land of their ancestors (Numbers 36:7).

This attachment to the land was fundamental, not only to their covenant relationship with God, but also to their wellbeing as a people. Russ Parker, in *Healing Wounded History*, says, 'One of the strongest and most basic needs of the whole human race is to belong, and to belong in the place or on the land where we can connect, be rooted and grow.' Paul, preaching in Athens, applies this principle to our spiritual wellbeing. **'From one man he made all the nations, that they should inhabit the whole earth; and he marked out their appointed times in history and the boundaries of their lands ...** *so that* **they would seek him and perhaps reach out for him and find him'** (Acts 17:26,27, italics mine).

Dave Bookless comments: 'It is in our long-term interaction with creation in a particular place that we find hints of God's glory and begin to seek for a relationship with God.' Even in exile in Babylon, the Lord, through Jeremiah, urges the people to put down roots and pray for the peace and prosperity of the city, **'because if it prospers, you too will prosper'** (Jeremiah 29:4–7). We were intended to be not only in relationship with God, but also with a local community and the natural world.

Included in the vision of the prophets concerning God's future renewal of his creation was the statement, **'Everyone will sit under their own vine and under their own fig tree'** (Micah 4:4). Every family would **'long enjoy the work of their hands'** (Isaiah 65:21–23). Gentiles would be included and have secure tenure of the land in this vision (Ezekiel 47:22,23).

An Amish proverb gives an interesting perspective on this: 'We didn't inherit the land from our fathers; we are borrowing it from our children.'

Care for the land

The most obvious example of the responsibility to care for the land lay in the command to allow it to lie fallow during each Sabbatical year and for two years during the time of Jubilee (Leviticus 25:4,5,11,12). Here we have a clear example of sustainable living — the need to maintain the health of the soil, not only for their own continued use, but also for future generations.

A similar example of the importance of providing for the continued productivity of the natural environment is the command not to take a mother bird with its young, so she can then lay a second brood (Deuteronomy 22:6,7). Another is that fruit trees were not to be harvested till the fourth year of growth (Leviticus 19:24). Nothing they can do in, on, or with the land is outside the sphere of God's moral inspection. From major issues of defence and national security down to how they grew their fruit trees, every area of life is included.

The observance of these laws obviously required a certain amount of faith, a willingness to trust God to provide sufficient food for their families for the Sabbatical year, or for two years in the case of Jubilee. He had promised to do this (Leviticus 25:18–22). This willingness would also be a factor in the release of bonded labourers with generous provision (Deuteronomy 15:12–18), the cancelling of debts (Deuteronomy 15:1–11), the limits to harvesting required in providing for the poor (Leviticus 19:9,10; Deuteronomy 24:19–22), the returning of houses to Levites and the banning of interest on loans to the poor (Leviticus 25:32–38). The motive God gives for this is his own generosity to his people in giving them the land (Leviticus 25:38). Indeed, some of the economic regulations called for the sacrifice of self-interest in favour of the needs of a fellow Israelite. As E W Heaton said in *The Hebrew Kingdoms*, the law was not designed 'for good business but for good community.'

It is significant that the Jubilee year was announced with a blast on the trumpet (the *yobel*, from which the name derives), an instrument associated with decisive acts of God. The return of Christ to announce the final Jubilee, when liberty is proclaimed to all his people and creation is renewed, is announced with the blowing of a trumpet (Matthew 24:31; 1 Corinthians 15:52; 1 Thessalonians 4:16; cf. Isaiah 27:12,13).

Neglect of the Sabbatical years is given as one of the causes of divine judgement: the prophets interpret the long exile in Babylon not only as judgement on Israel for widespread injustice and turning from the true worship of Yahweh, but also as an opportunity to help the land recover from hundreds of neglected Sabbatical years (Leviticus 26:32–35,42,43; 2 Chronicles 36:21; cf. Isaiah 24:1–7). 'I will remember the land,' Yahweh declared. When Nehemiah took over the governorship of returned exiles, one of his major concerns was to restore the divine covenant with the land (Nehemiah 5:1–13; 10:31). The covenant concerned the relationship between the human social order, divine blessing and the goodness of the land. The wellbeing of the land was inextricably tied up with faithfulness to the covenant. '**He turned rivers into a desert, flowing springs into thirsty ground, and fruitful land into a salt waste, because of the wickedness of those who lived there**' (Psalm 107:33,34). Their very presence in the land God had given them would depend on the manner in which they valued this gift. If they defiled the land, then '**it will vomit you out as it vomited our the nations that were before you**' (Leviticus 18:28). The prophet Habakkuk denounced the Babylonians for their destruction of nature as for their violence towards humans: '**The violence you have done to Lebanon will overwhelm you, and your destruction of animals will terrify you. For you have shed human blood; you have destroyed lands and cites and everyone in them**' (Habakkuk 2:17).

So many of the detailed instructions of the law refer to the use and care of the land, directly or indirectly, that this is easily the most comprehensive of the ethical and theological categories of the law. In *The Cosmic Covenant* Robert Murray reasons that there is a profound recognition of a precarious balance between created order and cosmic disorder running through the Hebrew Bible. He argues that the rituals and laws of the covenant community of Israel are designed to preserve and restore this order, in the face of those cosmic or human forces that threaten to disrupt or overwhelm it.

The right of all to the produce of the land

Adequate food was the right of everyone. The poor were permitted to feed on grapes in a neighbour's vineyard or to pluck grain when passing a field. Owners were obliged to leave part of their harvest for those in need as well as the tithe of the third year (Leviticus 19:9,10; Deuteronomy 26:12). The fallow land of the Sabbatical years and Jubilee provided food for the poor. '**An unploughed field produces food for the poor, but injustice sweeps it away**' (Proverbs 13:23). Land was not treated as a commercial resource, in a manner that so often leads to injustice in today's world, but as a means of blessing to be enjoyed by all.

This truth was stated by Pope John Paul II in his encyclical on 'Human work' (1981). He distanced himself from Marxist collectivism and liberal capitalism. In the latter case, he explained, the question is how 'the right to ownership of property is understood.' He continued:

> Christian tradition has never upheld this right as absolute and untouchable. On the contrary, it has always understood this right within the broader context of the right common to all to use the goods of the whole creation; *the right to private property is subordinated to the right to common use*, to the fact that goods are meant for everyone.

If we accept the premise that God's intention is that all have right to the produce of the land, then we must surely accept the truth of Michael Northcott's statement, 'Where wealth accrues to some such that this sustenance is denied to others then this is theft'. In Israel, the right of the poor to have access to the necessities of life had priority over the right of private ownership of property.

Respect for animal life

Israelite law enjoins a deep respect for life (Leviticus 17:13,14), exhibits what we would today call ecological consciousness (Deuteronomy 22:6,7), and conveys a passionate sense of what is right in dealing with fellow-creatures (Deuteronomy 14:21; cf. Genesis 49:5–7). Rebecca is chosen as wife for Isaac because she drew water for Abraham's camels, not just for his servant (Genesis 24:19). We have authority over and permission to make use of animals, but implicit in these is responsibility and accountability.

Fairness and compassion were commanded towards working animals, such as the laden donkey and threshing ox (Exodus 23:4,5; Deuteronomy 25:4; cf. 22:1–4). In the former instance, this had priority over feelings about a potential enemy. Domestic animals were included in the rest that was mandatory on the Sabbath, not only on the basis of God's example in creation (Exodus 20:11), but also on the grounds of his redemptive act (Deuteronomy 5:15). Wild animals were to benefit from the fallow land of the seventh year (Exodus 23:10,11).

A significant verse is Proverbs 12:10, '**The righteous care for the needs of their animals, but the kindest acts of the wicked are cruel.**' The word translated 'needs' here is *nephesh*, the Hebrew word for soul, and can refer to the inner, unspoken feelings and needs of human beings. Christopher Wright comments on this passage:

> The implications of this epigram are profound. Of the Hebrew
> virtues, the most all-embracing (*sedeq*) and the most deeply
> felt (*rahmim*), which are used of God towards humans and of
> humans towards each other, are here used in speaking of right
> and wrong attitudes towards animals. Thus animals are brought
> into the sphere of human ethics.

Of significance is the command in Deuteronomy 12:23,24 not to eat the blood of animals, '**because the blood is the life, and you must not eat the life with the meat ... Pour it out on the ground like water.**' This command was so important to the Jewish people that it was taken up by the early church as one of the restrictions imposed on the Gentiles (Acts 15:28,29).

Michael Northcott comments on the significance of this:

> The Hebrew Torah went this way many thousand of years before
> the modern animal rights movement. Instead of the language
> of rights it sets the treatment of animals in the context of their
> sharing of the divine-inspired character of all of life, and in terms
> of the responsibilities and duties which consequently arise for
> humans in their treatment of animals.

An emphasis on justice, particularly for the poor and disadvantaged

At the beginning of the creation God prepared his throne with justice, righteousness, faithfulness and love (Psalm 33:5,6; 89:12–15; 96:10,13). Ralph Knierim, in *The Task of Old Testament Theology*, says:

> The concern for justice pervades the entire Old Testament. It is
> found in the historical, legal, prophetic, and wisdom literature,
> and in the Psalms as well. It is found throughout the entire
> history of the Old Testament literature ... The evidence shows
> that the concern for justice was one, if not the central, factor
> by which ancient Israel's multifaceted societal life was united

> throughout its historical changes ... No sphere of Israel's life was
> exempt from concern for justice, and the Lord was known to be
> at work in all its spheres.

Righteousness and justice come in the top five of the Old Testament's
ethical vocabulary. Each of them, in various verbal, adjectival and noun
forms, occurs hundreds of times. Psalm 145 includes God's provision for
all his creatures in its definition of his *righteousness* as well as his love. It
places God's care for creation in precise parallel with his liberating acts
of justice for his people (vv. 13–17). '**The righteous care about justice for
the poor, but the wicked have no such concern**' (Proverbs 29:7).

Ideally, there should have been no poor (Deuteronomy 15:4),
considering the fair distribution of the land. However, humans being what
they are, greed, exploitation, laziness, incompetence and other factors
would inevitably result in a landless class of people. Israelite laws were
particularly concerned to protect them and addressed the needs of people
such as widows, orphans, immigrant foreigners and Levites (e.g. Leviticus
19:33; Deuteronomy 10:18; 12:19; 24:17) — precisely because such action
accords with God's character.

In the founding of the nation there were clear laws concerning justice
for all ranks of society. These included: the freedom of servants after
six years (Exodus 21:1–6); the forbidding of harsh working conditions
(Leviticus 25:39,40; 43); full and prompt payment of wages (Leviticus
19:13; Deuteronomy 24:14,15); respect for foreigners (Exodus 23:9);
fairness and impartiality in judicial matters (Exodus 23:6–8; Leviticus
19:15; Deuteronomy 16:19,20) and a mandatory rest on the Sabbath
for workers and even domestic animals (Exodus 20:11). There are 17
direct references to the forbidding of charging interest on loans to fellow
Israelites, particularly the needy (e.g. Deuteronomy 23:19; Exodus 22:25).
This was no doubt designed to prevent money becoming a commodity
that would begin the insidious process of diving the rich from the poor.
Economic generosity was commanded and reinforced by a mixture of
theological and economic arguments (e.g. Deuteronomy 15:12–15) and
the commands relating to the Sabbath and the Jubilee.

Slaves and other hired workers were permitted to enjoy all the benefits
of the great festivals and cultic occasions (e.g. Deuteronomy 16:11,14).
Such people would benefit from the triennial tithe (Deuteronomy

14:28,29). Though slavery was permitted in some circumstances, there were laws concerning the treatment of slaves that were unparalleled in any other Near Eastern code (Exodus 21:20,21,26,27; Deuteronomy 23:15,16). Slavery of fellow Israelites was forbidden (Leviticus 25:42; cf. Nehemiah 5:1–12; Job 31:13–15; Jeremiah 34:8–22; Amos 2:6).

Though not related to poverty in these particular instances, the laws relating to uncleanness, healthy diet, sanitary conditions and pollution are clearly most relevant today, though their application may vary with modern knowledge (see Leviticus 11–15, Deuteronomy 14; 23:9–14). Similarly, the forbidding of destruction of fruit trees in war is relevant (Deuteronomy 20:19).

Compassion toward foreigners was mandatory in view of their own experience. '**Do not oppress a foreigner; you yourselves know how it feels to be foreigners, because you were foreigners in Egypt**' (Exodus 23:9; cf. 22:21; Deuteronomy 15:15). They were even commanded to '**Love them as yourself**' (Leviticus 19:34). This is beautifully illustrated in the book of Ruth. Israel's society was geared towards the social health and economic viability of the 'lowest', not to the wealth, privilege or power of the 'highest'.

Power in decision-making, especially in judicial matters, resided in networks of elders. Such decentralised power stands in marked contrast to contemporary ancient Near Eastern states, which had highly stratified and pyramidical political and economic structures. According to Wolfram von Soden in *Ancient Orient*, 'After around 1500, there appear to have been only minimal institutional limitations on the power of the kings of Babylonia and Assyria.' If Israel was ever to appoint a king, which they eventually did against God's advice (1 Samuel 8), he was to read God's law '**all the days of his life**' so that he '**not consider himself better than his fellow Israelites**' (Deuteronomy 17:19,20).

Robert Gnuse's makes a noteworthy comment at the end of his survey of the Israelite laws and institutions relating to property in *You Shall Not Steal*:

> Laws and moral imperatives about loans, interest, debts, slaves, land, wages, justice in general indicate that the first concern of Israel was for human need, not ownership ... The maintenance

of property and possessions must come second to human need.
Israelites favoured persons over property and possessions.

God delights in kindness, justice and righteousness (Jeremiah 9:24),
and he made it clear that only through just living in their attitude to the
foreigner and the disadvantaged would he guarantee them a permanent
place in the land (Jeremiah 7:5–7). Jeremiah spoke this warning at a time
when God was about to send them into exile for 70 years!

Continued health of both the people and the land was inextricably
tied up with the worship of Yahweh, their God. Commenting in *Shalom*
on the combination of social, political and religious dimensions in the
clash between Yahweh and Baal at the time of Ahab and Elijah, Ulrich
Duchrow says, 'A starving people and a wealthy king is a result of the
law of the accumulation of riches and power, and happens when Ba'al
reigns and not Yahweh.' When things were not going well the only real
and lasting solution lay in repentance (2 Chronicles 7:14). Instead of the
hidden hand of the market, Donald Meek argues in *God the Economist:
The doctrine of God and political economy*, the Hebrew Bible proposes
God as the hidden hand who correlates abundance and gift with moral
righteousness and scarcity and famine with moral failure.

The community that God envisioned for his people was, in the words
of Paul Hansen in *People Called*, 'a people called by God, a community of
freed slaves within which the pyramid of social stratification consigning
certain classes to lives of ease and others to relentless suffering and
deprivation was to be banned forever.' For some time they more or less
succeeded. As Christopher Wright says:

> They succeeded for several centuries to prove, for example, that a
> theocracy could actually work without a human king; that land
> could be possessed and enjoyed without being treated merely
> as a commercial asset, to be bought, sold and exploited through
> absolute ownership; that a broad equality of families with built-
> in mechanisms for the prevention of poverty, debt and slavery
> could be maintained; that people's spiritual needs could be met
> without a highly consumptive, landowning, cultic elite.

Creation and the worship of Israel

Patrick Millar, in *Enthroned on the Praises of Israel: The praise of God in Old Testament theology*, says:

> To go through the Book of Psalms is to be led increasingly toward the praise of God as the final word ... that is so theologically, because in praise more than any other human act God is seen and declared to be God in all fullness and glory. That is so eschatologically, because the last word of all is the confession and praise of God by the whole creation.

The emphasis given to creation in the worship of Israel is most significant, and there is no better place to look for Israel's beliefs about God and about his creation, than in the Psalms. According to my reading of the Psalms, there are 71 that take some aspect of nature to illustrate a truth about life or about God. There are 42 that speak of God as the ruler, judge or possessor of all the nations or whole earth, or that he is to be worshipped by the whole earth. There are 44 that mention the fact that he is revealed in his creation, or that he is active in it, or that he possesses it, or is to be praised by it.

The Psalms of Asaph, in particular Psalms 74–79, display elements of rituals designed to preserve the order of heaven and earth and to sustain the blessings which come from God's covenant with his creation.

The temple, which was the central focus of their worship, was full of reminders of creation. Carvings of gourds, pomegranates, lilies, palm trees, flowers, lions, bears and bulls abounded. Some think the temple design was a depiction of the Garden of Eden. A major item was a huge bronze sculpture depicting the ocean, no doubt with waves and frolicking sea creatures amid the carved metallic swells.

The combined theme of creation and redemption is well illustrated by the six annual feasts of Israel. These began at Passover in their first month when they celebrated their deliverance from Egypt. This was to be replaced in the New Testament with the Lord's Supper as the time when Jesus gave himself for our sins. The Passover was immediately followed by the Feast of Firstfruits, which marked the beginning of the barley harvest, the earliest crop to ripen, when a sheaf from the harvest would be offered in the temple. At the commencement of the main harvest of other crops, seven weeks later, the Feast of Weeks was celebrated, which commemorated the arrival in Sinai and the giving of the Law. This combined the themes of redemption and creation, and new grain and two loaves baked from the first harvested wheat were presented in the temple. In the New Testament this corresponds to Pentecost, the beginning of the spiritual harvest, when 3000 souls were added to the fledgling church. No further feasts were held until the Feast of Trumpets on the first day of the seventh month. This was a celebration of the end of the harvest. The two final feasts, the Day of Atonement and the Feast of Tabernacles in the seventh month, returned again to the theme of redemption, with the emphasis on forgiveness and the deliverance from Egypt. These feasts are described in Leviticus 23. They were always celebrated with feasting, together with their families. It is noteworthy that there are constant commands to celebrate their worship with feasting and rejoicing (Deuteronomy 12:11,12; 14:22–27; 16:11,14; 26:11; 27:7). At the Feast of Tabernacles they were to rejoice for seven days (Leviticus 23:40)! It is significant that Israel has no feast today to celebrate the return from exile in Babylon in the sixth century. Though some did return to rebuild the temple, the complete restoration — as pictured by the prophet Isaiah, with the transformation of nature together with the full restoration of shalom blessings for God's people — has yet to occur, though the process was initiated with the coming of Jesus.

At all their celebrations, sacrifices would be made for forgiveness and reconciliation with their God, but these were always accompanied by offerings of grain, oil and wine — the fruits of the earth. Additional offerings from creation were their chief means of expressing gratitude to their God for his abundant provision of their needs. It is also significant that the reasons given for the command to rest on the Sabbath was both because of the completion of creation (Exodus 20:11) and their deliverance from Egypt (Deuteronomy 5:15). It was a day to remember both events with gratitude. As Leo Perdue sums it up in his book *Wisdom and Creation*, it is now clear to many scholars that 'Creation is a pervasive theme through every area of the Hebrew canon. The view that redemptive history … takes theological priority over creation cannot be defended by reference to the Hebrew Bible itself.' And as Larry Rasmussen notes:

> Religion in the Old Testament frequently seems hard to distinguish from good highlands agriculture, from proper

treatment of topsoil and animals, from joyful celebration over
bountiful harvests and the warm glow one gets from a goblet of
good wine.

All this emphasis shows how vital creation was to the Israelites. As long as
they maintained their faithfulness to their God, it is difficult to see how
they could not but value it and desire to care for it. As the history of Israel
makes plain, the health of the land was inextricably tied to their true
worship and the degradation of the land to its abandonment (cf. Haggai).

Though the application of the seven principles in this chapter may vary
from age to age and in different contexts, they are as relevant today as
ever, perhaps more so because of the situation to which we have brought
ourselves. It is true that Israel was primarily an agrarian society but there
are principles here that apply to any society.

Christopher Wright sums up as follows:

> Ancient Israel my not have been anxious or fearful about the
> plight of the physical planet in the way we are, for the very
> good reason that we have made a far greater mess of it than the
> ancient world ever did. So to that extent many aspects of what
> we would now regard as urgent ecological ethical issues were
> not explicitly addressed within the Old Testament. Nevertheless,
> the theological principles and ethical implications that they
> *did* articulate regarding creation do have a far-reaching impact
> on how biblically sensitive Christians will want to frame their
> ecological ethics today.

CHAPTER 11

Christ and creation

As we have seen, it was God's purpose from the beginning to come eventually in the person of his Son to complete all that he had initiated through the call of Abraham. Jesus, through his birth, life, death and resurrection, set in process the final act of the drama, which will be completed when he returns. In order to understand who Jesus really is and his relationship to creation, there is no better place to look than in the first chapter of Paul's letter to the Christians in Colossae. This is not the only place in the New Testament where Jesus is spoken of as the creator (e.g. John 1:1–14, 1 Cor 8:6, Heb 1:2,3,10), but, as this is the most concise and comprehensive passage on the subject in the New Testament, I will quote it in full.

> The Son is the image of the invisible God, the firstborn over all creation. For in him all things were created: things in heaven and on earth, visible and invisible, whether thrones or powers or rulers or authorities; all things have been created through him and for him. He is before all things, and in him all things hold together. And he is the head of the body, the church; he is the beginning and the firstborn from among the dead, so that in everything he might have the supremacy. For God was pleased to have all his fullness dwell in him, and through him to reconcile to himself all things, whether things on earth or things in heaven, by making peace through his blood shed on the cross.
>
> COLOSSIANS 1:15–20

Whatever it means for humans to be created in the image of God (and we have explored that above), Jesus, in his humanity, was the perfect example of that image. However, the above passage speaks of him as much more that that. Here he is presented as the source, the owner, the beneficiary, the sustainer and the redeemer of all creation. What is so remarkable about this passage is the repeated use of the word 'all'. Jesus is the firstborn over *all* creation. He is the creator of *all* things (mentioned twice). *All* things have been created for his benefit. He is before *all* things. He sustains *all* things. He has supremacy over *everything*. *All* God's fullness dwells in him. And he is the one who by his death reconciles *all* things to himself.

Richard Bauckham, in *Biblical Theology and the Problems of Monotheism*, points out the significance of this:

> Of the Jewish ways of characterising the divine uniqueness, the most unequivocal was by reference to creation. In the uniquely divine role of creating all things it was for Jewish monotheism unthinkable that any being other than God could even assist God (Isaiah 44:24; 4 Ezra 3:4 …) But to Paul's unparalleled inclusion of Jesus in the Shema [see 1 Corinthians 8:6; Deuteronomy 6:4] he adds the equally unparalleled inclusion of Jesus in the creative activity of God. No more unequivocal way of including Jesus in the unique divine identity is conceivable, within the framework of Second Temple Jewish monotheism.

As Irenaeus wrote in the third century, God crafted the world with the two hands of his Son and his Spirit.

Jesus shares authority over the universe with his Father. He is not only '**the ruler of the kings of the earth**' (Revelation 1:5), he is also '**the ruler of God's creation**' (Revelation 3:14). Both these statements could, of course, only be made about God. Through the miracles of turning the water into wine, stilling the storm, feeding the five and four thousands, and healing broken bodies and minds, he demonstrated this authority.

Note that the universe is created for Christ's benefit and enjoyment. Dave Bookless says, 'In a real and profound sense, the whole creation is God's love-gift to his Son, Jesus Christ. No wonder the universe is designed with such beauty and harmony. It is an expression of the love in the heart of God.'

Christ sustains the universe, and it is instructive to note creation's reaction to his crucifixion. As he hung on the cross the skies were darkened and at the moment of his death there was an earthquake flinging open tombs and tearing the curtain in the temple from top to bottom. Another earthquake occurred at his resurrection as nature responded in celebration to the beginnings of a new creation in Jesus' resurrection body.

Noteworthy, also, is the fact that it is all of creation that is to be reconciled through what Christ achieved by his death on the cross, and not just the world of humans.

James Dunn, in his concluding comment on this passage in *Epistles to the Colossians and to Philemon*, says:

> The vision is vast. The claim is mind-blowing. It says much for the faith of these first Christians that they should see in Christ's death and resurrection quite literally the key to resolving the disharmonies of nature and the inhumanities of humankind, that the character of God's creation and God's concern for the universe in its fullest expression could be so caught and encapsulated for them in the cross of Christ.

To quote Dunn again:

> What is being claimed is quite simply and profoundly that the divine purpose in the act of reconciliation and peacemaking was to restore the harmony of the original creation, to bring into renewed oneness and wholeness 'all things', 'whether things on the earth or things in the heavens.

A similar emphasis is found in Ephesians 1:10 where we are told it is God's purpose '**to bring unity to all things in heaven and earth under Christ.**' In 2 Corinthians 5, Paul declares that God not only reconciled us to himself through Christ (v. 18) but he was also reconciling the world (Greek: *kosmos)* to himself (v. 19). He goes on to explain that this message of reconciliation has been entrusted to us to proclaim as his ambassadors. Perhaps we can see significance in the fact that when the side of Jesus was pierced by the Roman soldier, his blood was poured on the earth for its healing, as was the blood of all the Old Testament sacrifices.

Paul concludes the passage in Colossians 1 on Christ and creation with the puzzling statement, '**This is the gospel that you heard and that has been proclaimed to every creature under heaven …**' (v. 23). Perhaps N T Wright's comment is relevant:

> What has happened in the death and resurrection of Christ, in
> other words, is by no means limited to its effects on those human
> beings who believe the gospel and thereby find new life here
> and hereafter. It resonates out, in ways that we can't fully see or
> understand, into the vast recesses of the universe.

This hope for the renewal of nature, together with the redemption of
God's people, is anticipated in the vision of the prophets (see Isaiah
11:6–9; 35; 65:17–25; Ezekiel 47:1–12; Hosea 2:14–23).

A further significant point is made by Wright in *Climax of the
Covenant*: 'The parallelism between its two halves [Colossians 1:15–20] …
invites the reader or listener to draw the conclusion that the creator is also
the redeemer, and vice versa.'

There are two main reasons in the Christian tradition as to why Jesus
became part of his own creation: to consecrate that creation, regardless
of sin, and to restore creation, because of sin. It is important that we
embrace both traditions. Paul Hansen says well: 'No goal short of the
resurrection of all of God's creation to its intended wholeness will satisfy
the yearning of the Servant of the Lord' (see Isaiah 40–66).

Colossians 1:15–20 focuses on the cross and does not mention the
resurrection. However, the resurrection is the guarantee of the final
restoration of all things. In itself it is the starting point of the final act of
that restoration. It is significant that a literal translation of Isaiah 65:17 is
'**Behold, I am creating a new heavens and a new earth.**' The process has
begun.

I referred earlier to the problem of the obvious suffering that we see
so much of in creation. How does this relate to the suffering of God
himself as it is so starkly revealed in the cross, particularly in reference to
the statement in Revelation 13:8 that Jesus was '**slain from the creation
of the world**'? In Philippians 2:7 Jesus is said to have '**made himself
nothing**'. The Greek word is *ekenōsen*, which could be translated 'emptied
(himself)'. It seems as if this self-emptying of God is not something that
began at Calvary, but is inherent in the very nature of God himself and is
inextricably linked with the whole of creation. Jürgen Moltmann suggests
this in his book *God in Creation*:

> God withdraws himself, steps back, limits himself in order to
> make creation possible. God's creative activity outwards is

preceded by this humble divine self-restriction. In this sense,
God's self-humiliation does not begin merely with creation,
in as much as God commits himself to this world; it begins
beforehand and is the presupposition that makes creation
possible. God's creative act is grounded in his humble, self-
humiliating love. This self-restricting love is the beginning
of that self-emptying of God, which Philippians 2 sees as the
divine mystery of the precise purpose of the Messiah. Even in
order to create heaven and earth God emptied himself of his all-
plenishing omnipotence, and as Creator took upon himself the
form of a servant.

Loren Wilkinson, speaking at the Creation Groaning Conference held at
Regent College, Vancouver, cites Holmes Rolston, associate editor of the
highly respected *Journal of Environmental Ethics*. He describes Rolston
as 'having written eloquently on the pattern of what he calls kenosis in
nature, the self-giving that is evident throughout, willingly or not, in
creatures. It is not altruism, yet there is a sense in which creatures live in
and though others. It is particularly evident in the salmon run where the
salmon struggle upstream for the sole purpose of giving their life for their
offspring.' Rolston says:

> Nature is cruciform. Life is advanced through suffering and
> pathos. The cruciform creation is in the end deiform, godly,
> because of this element of struggle, not in spite of it. There is
> a great divine 'Yes' hidden behind and within every 'No' of
> crushing nature. God rescues from suffering, but the Judeo-
> Christian faith never avoids suffering in the achievement of his
> divine purpose. To the contrary, seen in the paradigm of the
> cross, God too suffers, not less than the creatures, in order to
> gain for the creatures a more abundant life.

Again he says:

> Everywhere there is vicarious suffering. The global earth is a
> land of promise, and yet has to be died for. The story is a passion
> play, long before it reaches Christ. Since the beginning, myriad
> creatures have been giving up their lives as a ransom for many.
> In that sense, Jesus is not an exception to the natural order, but a
> chief exemplification of it.

CS Lewis says something similar in *Miracles*. Speaking of the widespread recognition throughout the world that somehow death and life are intimately connected, Lewis says of that pattern that 'It is derived through human imagination, from the facts of nature, and the facts of nature from her Creator. The death and rebirth pattern is in her, because it was first in him, the Lamb slain from the foundation of the world.'

I don't profess to understand all this, yet I am sure there is a profound truth here. There is a real sense in which God suffers with his creation, and this is language we tend to avoid in the church. As Wilkinson says, 'Self-giving suffering love is central to who God is ... The Creator pours himself out for his creation from the beginning in a self-giving which culminates in the Cross.'

The reason Paul speaks of Christ's self-emptying in Philippians 2 is to underline that we should have a similar attitude. '**In your relationship with one another, have the same attitude of mind Christ Jesus had**' (Philippians 2:5). Applying this to our attitude to creation, Rolston says:

> We can envisage the possibility of kenosis, self-emptying, in a still richer sense, where self-interested humans impose limits on human welfare on behalf of other species. Humans are distinguished by their ability to see others, to oversee a world. Environmental ethics advances beyond the usual Christian ethics in that it considers others before humans. We can put this provocatively by saying that Christian kenosis is called to rise to sufficient moral vision to count real others, non-humans, trees, species, ecosystems. The secular world looks for the management of nature, for reducing all nature to human resources, and plans a technology and industry to accomplish that in the next century and millennium, but, in that aspiration, humans only escalate their inherited desires for self-actualisation, tempted now into self-aggrandisement on scales never before possible. The Christian opportunity today is to limit such human aggrandisement on behalf of the five million other species that also reside on earth.

It is significant that the *physical territory* of Palestine is nowhere referred to with any theological significance in the New Testament. Instead, all the vocabulary of blessing, holiness, promise, gift, inheritance and so on, which is associated with the land in the Old Testament, is applied to

Christ himself. One may well get the impression from this that land is of no more importance. However, this is far from the case. Christopher Wright explains this as follows:

> This is partly because the Christian churches rapidly spread beyond its borders to other lands throughout the Mediterranean and beyond. But much more importantly it is because the holiness of the land, and indeed all its other attributes in the Old Testament thinking, was transferred to Christ himself. The spiritual presence of the living Christ sanctifies any place where believers are present. This transference of the holiness of the land to Christ is well presented by W D Davies, who points out how Christianity reacted to all the concrete details of Judaism, including the land, 'in terms of Christ, to whom all places and all space, like all things else, are subordinated. In sum, for the holiness of place, Christianity has fundamentally … substituted the holiness of the Person: it has Christified holy space.'* The promise of Jesus to be present wherever his people meet, effectively universalises the Old Testament promise of God's presence among his people in the land, for now the people of Jesus are everywhere.

William Cowper expressed this beautifully in a hymn he wrote for his congregation when they had to move to a new building for worship:

> Jesus where'er thy people meet
> There they behold thy mercy seat
> Where'er they seek thee, thou art found
> And every place is hallow'd ground.

Another point worth noting is Jesus' constant reference to himself as the Son of Man. This is normally believed to be an allusion to the 'son of man' mentioned by the prophet Daniel (7:13). This is no doubt true enough. However, 'Son of Man' is literally 'Son of Adam', the one who was created from the dust of the earth. Jesus is talking about himself as 'the son of the one hewn from the earth' as James Jones puts it in *Jesus and the Earth*. Perhaps we could call him 'son of the soil'. Adam's disobedience had its adverse effect on human relationships with nature. Jesus, as the perfect image of the invisible God, is our perfect model for caring for nature.

---

* W D Davies, *Gospel and the Land*.

CHAPTER 12

The Church and creation

It is very significant that God puts the responsibility for taking the lead in bringing healing to the land squarely on his own people, which in New Testament terms are those who have put their trust in his Son, Jesus Christ, and claim to be his followers. And the first step we are required to take is that of repentance. '**If my people, who are called by my name, will humble themselves and pray and seek my face and turn from their wicked ways, then I will hear from heaven, and I will forgive their sin and will heal their land**' (2 Chronicles 7:14). Having acknowledged our failures to care for the planet he has entrusted to us, we will demonstrate our true repentance in what we choose to do about it. There are three areas of its life in which I believe the church needs to give attention to creation: its worship, its teaching and its outreach to the community.

Worship

As the central act of worship in the church is the Eucharist, or Lord's Supper, the only religious ceremony specifically commanded by our Lord apart from baptism, it is important that we explore its connection with environmental issues. The main focus of the Lord's Supper is on the cross and its benefits. '**This is my blood of the covenant, which is poured out for many for the forgiveness of sins**' (Matthew 26:28). As we have seen, it is by means of the cross that not only humans are reconciled to God, but also the whole of creation is to be renewed in perfect relationship with its creator. This being the case, it should be fully recognised in both our eucharistic liturgies and the manner in which we celebrate it.

In ancient Israel, practically all religious festivals included recognition of God's provision through his gifts of the fruits of the earth. This understanding was evident in offerings and liturgies, but most significantly through feasting and festivities and the emphasis on sharing good things with the poor and the stranger. This emphasis on the sacred value of communal meals is taken over into the New Testament. Some of Jesus' most significant teaching moments occurred in the contexts of meals (Matthew 9:10–13; Mark 14:3–9; Luke 7:36–50; 14:1–23; John 2:1–12; 6:1–15; 25–59). It was on these occasions particularly that he demonstrated his love for the sinner and outcast, illustrating the chief purpose of his mission. His favourite metaphor for the kingdom of God was that of a banquet, particularly a wedding banquet, which is the most joyful of all human celebrations (Matthew 22:1–14; 25:1–13; Luke 14:15–23). Eating together is no doubt one of the most effective ways of building community.

Jesus' final instructions to his disciples, the night before he was crucified, occurred over a meal, probably a Jewish Passover meal. John devotes five chapters to describing all that he taught them on this occasion (John 13–17). It was in the context of this meal that he took two of the most common symbols of the good fruits of the earth, '**wine that gladdens humans hearts … and bread that sustains their hearts**' (Psalm 104:15), to speak of his coming death and its purpose, our forgiveness (Matthew 26:28).

We only have one description in the New Testament of a celebration by Christians of the Lord's Supper (1 Corinthians 11:17–34). Paul refers to it because of the misuse the Corinthians were making of it, but it gives us clues as to the nature of early Christian gatherings. It took place in the context of an ordinary meal to which all local believers, of all ranks of society, were welcome and at which food was shared. At some point of the meal thanksgiving would be made for the death and resurrection of the Saviour through the breaking of bread and the sharing of wine. No doubt there would be a time set aside for teaching, maybe during the meal, with discussion invited. I am sure that celebration of the creation and the good fruits of the earth, as so evident in the Psalms of Israel, would have also been included.

Today, we have so formalised the Lord's Supper that the communal aspect, which is so prominent in the teaching of Paul, is downplayed, and the emphasis on the good gifts of creation barely get a mention. It would be great to see a return to this feasting aspect of the celebration of this central act of our worship, in recognition of the significance of creation and in anticipation of the **'wedding supper of the Lamb'**, when we **'take [our] places at the feast with Abraham, Isaac and Jacob in the kingdom of heaven'** (Revelation 19:9; Matthew 8:11). The medieval practice of the presentation of the 'holy loaf', whereby a different family from the congregation makes the bread by hand each week from flour that has been sustainably grown, and brings it to church to become the loaf that is broken and shared around, is a step in the right direction. It is still practised in some parts of Europe, but in my opinion does not go nearly far enough. Even having a 'potluck' meal after the worship is over does not recover the emphasis of the early church, when the service of the Word was organised *around* the meal, rather than tacking the meal on when the liturgy is over. If we can recover the sacredness of eating together as God's people, whether in our church gatherings or our homes, maybe we will begin to give more consideration to the manner in which the food is grown, marketed and presented. Joachim Jeremias, in *New Testament Theology*, has this to say about table fellowship in an eastern setting:

> It is important to realise that in the east, even today, to invite a man to a meal is an honour. It was an offer of peace, trust, brotherhood and forgiveness; in short, sharing a table meant sharing life … In Judaism in particular, table-fellowship means fellowship before God.

It is my conviction that the **'body of Christ'** which Paul refers to in 1 Corinthians 11:29, and which the Corinthians were failing to recognise by their treatment of the poor, was not the material or mystical body of Christ represented by the broken bread, but the body of the Christian fellowship which Paul describes in such detail in the following chapter. This was the belief of those Christian farmers who left severe persecution in Europe and established the Anabaptist community in North America. For them it was not the priest or the altar, nor their mystical association with Christ, which made the elements of bread and wine holy, but rather the gathering of the whole people of God and the holiness of lives. It is the quality of our fellowship that makes the eating and drinking worthy or otherwise (1 Corinthians 11:27).

As Michael Northcott suggests, the Anabaptist recognition of the foundational significance of Christian eating is surely not unconnected with their resistance to modern agricultural practices. Their lack of debt to banks and government for high inputs of machinery and chemicals, and their contentment with growing sufficient for their communities, have made them not only the best conservers of soil in North America, but also its most successful farmers, if success is measured by quality of life as well as quantity of production. Michael Northcott adds:

> In such ways it turns out once again that acts of resistance to the global economy and its destruction of a stable climate through global warming are not a costly burden, but instead involve the joyful recovery of forms of life that industrialism has sacrificed on the altar of surplus value.

Contemporary liturgists, such as Episcopalian priest Scott McCarthy, have created eucharistic and seasonal prayers and rites, ceremonies of light and darkness, rituals in the open air and forms of thanksgiving for water, minerals, animals and food designed to remake connections to place and land, time and seasons which the church has lost, especially since the Industrial Revolution. We must learn to make creative use of such resources in our worship. It is significant, as noted earlier, that in the worship around the throne of God in Revelation 4 and 5, praise for creation comes before praise for redemption.

On an individual level, it is good to take such opportunities as we have to both enjoy and meditate on the wonders of creation. John Calvin once wrote:

> There is no doubt that the Lord would have us uninterruptedly occupied in holy meditation; that while we contemplate in all creatures, as in mirrors, his wisdom, justice, goodness, and power, we should not merely run over them cursorily and, so to speak, with a fleeting glance; but we should ponder them at length, turn them over in our minds seriously and faithfully, and recollect them repeatedly. For there are as many miracles of divine power ... as there are kinds of things in the universe.

As the hymn puts it:

Joy to the world! The Lord is come;
Let earth receive her King;
Let every heart prepare him room,
And heaven and nature sing.

That's good theology and good worship.

Teaching

How often does one hear a sermon, or even a series of sermons, on the
importance of creation and our responsibility to value and care for it?
It is my hope that this book may be a useful resource for such teaching,
whether in sermons or study groups. There are some relevant subjects
that may be beyond the expertise of a local congregation but where this
is the case we can invite qualified Christians to give input to our regular
gatherings. According to theologian Jürgen Moltmann, the neglect of
economics is 'a wound in the side of the Church.'

Outreach

The church is becoming increasingly aware that demonstrating care for
God's planet is as significant in this modern world as caring for the people
in it. In fact, the two are often inextricably connected. Demonstrating
God's love for his creation by our actions can provide links with others
who have similar concerns, though perhaps with different motives, and
can have a powerful evangelistic result. Christopher Wright has this to say:

> The gospel is indeed good news for the whole of creation. It is not
> surprising then that those who take seriously, as Christians, our
> responsibility to embody God's love for creation find that their
> obedience in that sphere often leads to opportunities to articulate
> God's love for suffering and lost people also. The story of
> A Rocha has shown that while the movement's goals and actions
> in creation care have their own intrinsic validity, God honours
> such obedience by blessing and building his church as well in the
> context of such activity.
>
> Truly Christian environmental action is in fact also
> evangelistically fruitful, not because it is any kind of cover for
> 'real mission' but simply because it declares in word and deed
> the Creator's limitless love for the whole of his creation (which
> of course includes his love for his human creatures) and makes

no secret of the biblical story of the cost that the Creator paid to redeem both.

Dave Bookless says of his experience in A Rocha:

> We are not using environmental work as an excuse to smuggle in the 'real' spiritual gospel. Instead, we are living out and sharing all that God has called us to: our part in God's mission to the world. This is what seems to attract those who are searching for spiritual reality, which makes sense in a world of damaged people and degraded ecosystems.

Though we must be prepared to work with any group that is doing good environmental work, regardless of individuals' personal beliefs, there is a real place for specifically Christian organisations to demonstrate on a wider scale what Christians are about and why.

The evangelist Dr Rob Frost has said, 'When Christians take the earth seriously, people take the gospel seriously.'

Romans 8:19 states: '**The creation waits in eager expectation for the children of God to be revealed.**' No doubt this has a primary reference to the future renewal of creation. Maybe creation is also waiting for us to be revealed as its primary caretakers in the present.

There are so many things that can and need to be done to restore some of the natural environments and ecosystems of this planet and, at the very least, to prevent things from getting worse. We all have different gifts and different opportunities and it is up to each to decide what we can do individually and collectively. The task may seem enormous, but we can do something. As the saying goes, 'How do you eat an elephant?' 'One bite at a time!'

Numerous websites offer suggestion and tell us what is already being done. On a personal level, I like the six Rs:

- **Reduce** our consumption of non-essentials to healthy living.
- **Reuse** where possible to reduce waste.
- **Recycle** — this is what God does.
- **Resist** the temptations that abound in our materialistic society.
- **Restore** what has been lost where that is possible.

■ **Rejoice** in the goodness of God in all that he has made and all he provides.

Poet Gary Snyder, when asked what to do to stem the tide of ecological degradation and work to improve the state of our home planet, said, 'Settle down, get to know your place, and dig in.'

However, we can achieve much more if we can work together on specific projects with likeminded people. Many churches are developing programmes to make their own churches environmentally friendly, and also tackling specific programmes in their communities. I recently read of a Tanzanian pastor who encouraged all the churches in his region to establish tree nurseries. They required those going through confirmation classes to plant trees in order to graduate. As a result, over 500,000 trees have been planted, and an important water source that had become intermittent now flows steadily.

We can support our own churches in such activities, but also, where it fits our gifts and interests, join an informal group working on some environmental project, or an organisation such as A Rocha. There is a very significant movement in Christian colleges across the United States as staff and students become more aware of the fact that care of creation is a justice issue and necessary for helping people. Those involved in business communities can exert their influence there.

And we will achieve much more if we recognise this is God's work and we depend on him. Mary Magdalene, after Jesus' resurrection, thought he was the gardener. Actually, she got it right. He is the Head Gardener and calls us to work with him. He has come to uproot the thorns and thistles and plant myrtle and cypress instead, as Isaiah foretold.

And Wendell Berry reminds us in *Sabbaths* that the responsibility for the final outcome of our work is not ours alone:

> Whatever is foreseen in joy
> Must be lived out from day to day.
> Vision held open in the dark
> By our ten thousand days of work.
> Harvest will fill the barn; for that
> The hand must ache, the face must sweat.
>
> And yet no leaf of grain is filled
> By work of ours, the field is tilled

And left to grace. That we may reap,
Great work is done while we're asleep.

When we work well, a Sabbath mood
Rests on our day and finds it good.

Joseph Santmire concludes his book *Nature Reborn* with these words:

> Life as a Christian has never been easy. Nor should it be any
> easier today. But, shaped by its ecological and cosmic ritual
> enactments, and buoyed by its now ecological and cosmic
> spirituality, this martyr church can rise to this historic occasion
> today, by the grace of God, to respond to what is perhaps an
> unprecedented calling, to love God and all God's creatures, as
> one great and glorious extended family, and in so doing to be a
> light to the nations and a city set upon a hill, whose exemplary
> witness cannot be hidden.

Eugene Peterson's appealing translation of Philippians 2:15 in *The Message* suggests we can make a difference: 'Go into the world uncorrupted, a **breath of fresh air in this squalid and polluted society. Provide people with a glimpse of good living and of the living God.**'

CHAPTER 13

The renewal of creation

There are a number of passages in the Bible which make it clear that Peter's statement that God would '**restore everything, as he promised long ago through the holy prophets**' (Acts 3:21) includes the restoration not only of humans but of the whole creation. This has been insisted on by many prominent theologians down the ages, from Irenaeus and Augustine through Luther, Calvin and Wesley. We have seen that the cross is effective for the reconciliation of '**all things, whether things on earth or things in heaven, by making peace through his blood, shed on the cross**' (Colossians 1:20). Ronald Sider, commenting on this passage in an article in *Christianity Today*, says, 'That does not mean that everyone will be saved; rather it means that Christ's salvation will finally extend to all of creation.' Four times the Bible speaks of 'a new heavens and a new earth' (Isaiah 65:17; 66:22; 2 Peter 3:13; Revelation 21:1). Note that Peter adds it will be an earth and heaven '**where righteousness dwells**' (2 Peter 3:13). All taint of sin and evil will be removed. Goodness and love will reign supreme.

As Peter stated, there are glimpses of this in the prophets of the Old Testament. Hosea foretold that in messianic times God's covenant with his people would include '**the beasts of the field, the birds in the sky and the creatures that move along the ground**' (Hosea 2:18; cf. Isaiah 41:18–20; 55:12,13; Amos 9:13; Micah 4:3,4). Both Hosea and the Psalmist use the analogy of marriage, using the technical language of nuptial consent and acceptance, namely, 'respond' and 'answer', to illustrate the depth of the relationships that will exist between God, his people and creation (Hosea 2:21–23; Psalm 85:10–13). Isaiah's magnificent vision of the return and restoration of his people in chapter 35 includes the restoration of nature. I suspect that his statement that 'The wolf will live with the lamb, the leopard will lie down with the goat, the calf and the lion and the yearling together; and a little child will lead them ...' (Isaiah 11:6–9) will be more literally fulfilled than we could imagine.

If our vision of the future is a rather vague disembodied state that has no place for trees, flowers, mountains, lakes, and fascinating animals and insects, then it is likely that we will not attach much value to them in the present. Anthony Hoekema, in *The Bible and the Future*, even went so far as to say that to envisage the new kingdom as anything other than a renewed creation would be to concede a great victory to the devil.

> If God would have to annihilate the present cosmos ... then Satan would have succeeded in so devastatingly corrupting the present cosmos and the present earth that God could do nothing with it but blot it totally out of existence.

It is significant that it is in the wilderness that Isaiah predicts the Messiah will begin his ministry. 'A voice of one calling: "In the wilderness prepare the way for the Lord, make straight in the desert a highway for the Lord"' (Isaiah 40:3). This verse is quoted by all four gospels. In the imagery of Isaiah the wilderness was not a place of delightful flowers but of thorns and briers, a place where scorpions sting and vultures feed on carcasses of the dead. It was not a place where birds sing, trees clap their hands and rivers leap to praise God. It is here that Jesus begins his work of re-creation. Maybe there is significance in the fact that, right at the beginning of his ministry, Jesus 'was in the wilderness ... with the wild animals' (Mark 1:13). Interestingly, there is an ancient Jewish document from about that time called 'The Life of Adam and Eve'. In chapter 19, verses 13 and 14, it talks about Adam taking the role of a penitent and standing in the river Jordan for 40 days surrounded by the beasts. The animals come to him as he prays for the restoration of creation.

Loren Wilkinson says:

> [Christians] are rediscovering the truth that redemption is not human salvation *out of* a doomed creation, but rather the *restoration* of all God's purposes in creation. Theological support for this view comes from theologians as diverse as Irenaeus in the second century and John Calvin in the sixteenth ... In ways

we hardly understand, it will be the human privilege to complete
creation and be its voice of praise to the Creator.

The Bible is clear that we go to 'be with Christ' at death where we enjoy
his presence in a state that is 'better by far' (Philippians 1:23) than the
trials of this life, but this is only half the story. One day he is returning in
glory as the New Testament repeatedly states. Then there will come our
resurrection to new bodies that are imperishable, glorious, powerful and
spiritual (1 Corinthians 15:42–44). Then also will come the restoration of
all creation (Acts 3:21). So we must stop talking as if 'going to heaven' is
the ultimate goal of the Christian. John's magnificent vision of the future
in Revelation 21 and 22 takes place on earth, not in heaven. 'I saw the
holy city, the new Jerusalem, coming down out of heaven from God,
prepared as a bride beautifully dressed for her husband. And I heard a
loud voice from the throne saying, "Look! God's dwelling place is now
among the people, and he will dwell with them. They will be his people,
and God himself will be with them and be their God"' (Revelation
21:2,3). Note that God comes to dwell with us, not we with him. (It is the
same Greek word that John uses of Jesus dwelling among us in John 1:14).
It is not as in the story of the tower of Babel when people sought to reach
for God. It is the *earth* that 'will be full of the knowledge of the Lord as
the waters cover the sea' (Isaiah 11:9). Christopher Wright sums up the
Biblical emphasis as follows:

> The consistent biblical hope, from Genesis to Revelation is that
> God should do something with the *earth* so that we can once
> again dwell upon it in 'rest', in Sabbath peace with him. The Bible
> speaks predominantly of the need for God to come here, not of
> the wish for us to go somewhere else. This earth is to be the place
> of God's judgement, and also the place of God's saving power.
> So the flood story and its sequel becomes the sign not only of
> God's commitment to life on earth while it lasts (in the covenant
> tied up with its rainbow ribbon) but also of the coming final
> judgment and renewal — the new creation.

As Larry Rasmussen said in a lecture given at St Olaf College, the reason
the prophets ultimately predict our beating swords into ploughshares is
not only to end bloody warfare on the earth, but also to enable us to return
to our true calling: earthkeeping — tending the garden of God's creation!

All this was guaranteed by the resurrection of Jesus when his *material* body was transformed, issuing in the beginning of the new age. NT Wright expresses this emphasis eloquently and forcefully in his timely book *Surprised by Hope*. In an interview in *Christianity Today* he says:

> The Western Church has been fixated on going to heaven and has lost its grip on the resurrection and on the embodiedness of the future life. When I worked at Westminster Abbey I noticed that tombstones before about 1780 or so would often say things about the resurrection: 'I'm resting here at the moment but I'll be back, I shall arise.' Through the 19th century and on into the 20th century you don't get that. Instead you get: 'Gone home to be with Jesus' or 'Heaven is home'. It's important to give comfort to people so they know that the loved one who died is with Jesus, but the whole of the New Testament insists that's not the end of the story. There will be a new day, a new world, a new creation and new bodies to live in it. When you say this, people sort of scratch their heads and say, 'Yeah, I guess I sort of believe that but I really thought it was just about going to heaven.' It's really time to get a grip because it affects everything else: how we do ethics, how we do politics, it plays out in a whole range of things.

It is time we rethought the message of hymns such as the following:

> This world is not my home, I'm just passing through.
> My treasures are laid up somewhere beyond the blue.
> The angels beckon me from Heaven's open door
> And I can't feel at home in this world anymore.

When Jacob had his vision of a ladder connecting earth and heaven and the Lord promised to give him the land on which he had slept, he had the sense to declare, '**this is none other than the house of God; *this* is the gate of heaven**' (Genesis 28:17, italics mine).

A little over 100 years ago, an American pastor in upstate New York celebrated in a great hymn both the beauty of creation and the presence of the creator God within it. His name was Maltbie Babcock, and his hymn 'This is my Father's world' points beyond the present beauty of creation, through the mess and tragedy with which it has been infected, to the ultimate resolution. There are different versions of the relevant stanza, but this one is the clearest:

This is my Father's world; O let me ne'er forget
That though the wrong seems oft so strong,
God is the ruler yet.
This is my Father's world; The battle is not done;
Jesus who died, shall be satisfied,
And earth and heaven be one.

Paul's view

The most striking and comprehensive statement of all concerning the restoration of creation is that of Paul in Romans 8:16–26, which is worth quoting in full.

> The Spirit himself testifies with our spirit that we are God's children. Now if we are children, then we are heirs — heirs of God and co-heirs with Christ, if indeed we share in his sufferings in order that we may also share in his glory. I consider that our present sufferings are not worth comparing with the glory that will be revealed in us. The creation waits in eager expectation for the children of God to be revealed. For the creation was subjected to frustration, not by its own choice, but by the will of the one who subjected it, in hope that the creation itself will be liberated from its bondage to decay and brought into the freedom and glory of the children of God.
>
> We know that the whole creation has been groaning as in the pains of childbirth right up to the present time. Not only so, but we ourselves, who have the firstfruits of the Spirit, groan inwardly as we wait eagerly for our adoption, the redemption of our bodies. For in this hope we were saved. …
>
> In the same way, the Spirit helps us in our weakness. We do not know what we ought to pray for, but the Spirit himself intercedes for us through wordless groans.

I am much indebted to a talk by biblical scholar Gordon Fee, given at the Creation Groaning Conference at Regent College, Vancouver, for the basic outline of what follows.

The most remarkable thing about this passage is the way Paul links the present situation and future destiny of humans with that of the whole creation. He does this in a number of ways. Both humans and creation are waiting for our final glory. We 'wait eagerly' for it (v. 23), while the creation also '**waits in eager expectation**' (v. 19). The Greek word Paul uses here is a rare one in the Bible (*apokaradokia*), but it is an expressive one because it literally refers to a 'craning of the neck.' It is as if creation is standing on tiptoe, stretching it neck to catch a glimpse of its final restoration. Both are in bondage to decay (vv. 21). It is because of this that we wait for the transformation of our present bodies (23). Both are said to 'groan' because of our present condition (vv. 22,23), as does the Spirit (v. 26). The creation groans '**as in the pains of childbirth**' (v. 22) — a well-known Jewish metaphor for the emergence of God's new age — and we also '**groan inwardly**' (v. 23). Both have '**hope**' of future glory (vv. 20,24). The form that this glory will take for both humans and nature is described as that of liberation '**into glorious freedom**' (v. 21). This liberation will no doubt mean different things for different parts of the planet, whether it be liberation from grinding poverty, destructive lifestyles or other things that impact the environment. Scott Hoezee comments, 'Hope has been spread onto the soil of this earth like a good fertiliser. Its runoff seeps into every lake and river and ocean and is sucked up into every tree and cornstalk, and billows through the clouds in the sky.'

Another significant point is the number of times Paul uses words that begin with the Greek suffix *sun-*, meaning 'with'. This is not always obvious in English translations. In verse 16 the Spirit bears witness *with* our spirit that we are God's children. In verse 17 we are co-heirs *with* Christ, we suffer *with* Christ, and we will be glorified *with* Christ. In verse 22 the creation groans *with* us and suffers in childbirth *with* us (implied — the creation does not groan with itself). In verse 26 the Spirit comes alongside *with* us to help us in our praying. The relationships that have existed between the Father, Son and Spirit from all eternity will be extended to include all of God's children together with the whole of creation.

A further significant emphasis is the role played by the Spirit. This chapter is one of the significant passages in scripture concerning the ministry of the Spirit. He is mentioned 19 times. In these verses (16–26) he is the one who confirms our relationship with God as his children, and therefore co-heirs with Christ of his kingdom, which includes the whole of creation. As the firstfruits, he confirms our final adoption when our bodies will be redeemed (v. 23) and will be the one who raises us from the dead as he raised Jesus from the dead (Romans 1:4). In the present he 'helps us in our weakness' (v. 26).

The question arises as to whom Paul is referring when he speaks of the one who subjected creation to frustration. Was it Adam through his disobedience, or God? I tend to go with statement of *The Expositor's Greek Testament*: '[It] seems best referred to God: it was on account of Him — that His righteousness might be shown in the punishment of sin — that the sentence fell upon man, carrying consequences which extended to the whole realm, intended originally for his dominion.' Paul seems to have Genesis 3 in mind as he links human suffering and need for redemption with the frustrations of creation. We know that human sin is responsible for much that seems awry in creation, but not all. Paul does not make distinctions here and we do well to admit the limitations of our knowledge. However, Paul does appear to put the ultimate responsibility on God. But note that the creation is subject to frustration **'in hope'** (v. 20).

Before leaving Romans 8, it is worth comparing this passage with 1 Corinthians 6:12–20. The Corinthians had an attitude to the human body bordering on Gnosticism. Their slogan was **'food for the stomach and the stomach for food, and God will destroy them both'** (v. 13). What you did with the body was unimportant, as it will be destroyed anyway. The body didn't count. That gave freedom to go to the prostitute. Paul contradicts this with two arguments. First, the body belongs to the Lord, united with him in spirit, and therefore destined for resurrection, not destruction. It has been purchased by him at great price. Second, it has become the sacred temple of the Holy Spirit. We are not free to do as we wish with our bodies but duty bound to honour God with them. In 1 Corinthians 9:24–27, he adds the importance of discipline, treating our bodies as servant, not master.

In Romans 8:23 Paul speaks about **'the redemption of our bodies'.** This comes at the culmination of Paul's discussion in the first eight chapters of Romans concerning our redemption. It is very likely that we see here the reason he includes his comments about creation at this point. As our material bodies are included in our redemption, so is the material environment in which we live. And if we are to treat our bodies with reverence now because they belong to the Lord and will one day share his glory, surely we must care for creation now for exactly the same reasons.

I believe this to be the most powerful argument for caring for creation in the present that we have in the New Testament.

2 Peter 3:10-13

One passage of scripture that deserves some comment, as it has led to much misunderstanding among Christians, is 2 Peter 3:10–13: '**But the day of the Lord will come like a thief. The heavens will disappear with a roar; the elements will be destroyed by fire, and the earth and everything done in it will be laid bare. Since everything will be destroyed in this way, what kind of persons ought you to be? You ought to live holy and godly lives as you look forward to the day of God and speed its coming. That day will bring about the destruction of the heavens by fire, and the elements will melt with heat. But in keeping with his promise we are looking forward to a new heaven and a new earth, where righteousness dwells.**'

Many Christians have taken the attitude that since this present world is to be destroyed, what is the point of taking care of it? Quite apart from all the reasons for caring for this planet that we have so far discussed, this attitude depends on a questionable interpretation of the passage. Instead of 'will be laid bare' in verse 10, the KJV and NASB translations have 'will be burned up'. This is a translation of the Greek word *katesetai*. However, the oldest and most reliable Greek manuscripts do not have *katesetai* but *heurethêsetai* (reflected in both the United Bible Society and the Nestle-Aland Greek New Testaments), which has the meaning of finding or discovering. Our word 'eureka' comes from it. It is translated '**will be laid bare**' in the TNIV (above), the NIV and the NEB. The NRSV has '**will be disclosed**'. Richard Bauckham's interpretation – that the earth and everything in it will be 'found out', that is, exposed and laid bare before God's judgement so that the wicked and all their works will no longer be able to hide or find any protection – seems to be what this passage is all about. The earth will not be totally destroyed, but purified, resulting in a 'new' earth. God will not make 'all new things', but 'all things new' (Revelation 21:5).

An apt illustration is that of a forest fire, after which new green shoots spring up from the scorched earth. C S Lewis painted a great picture of this in the conclusion of *The Chronicles of Narnia*. Aslan takes the children into a new world. Following a great conflagration of fire and wind they see a world strangely familiar and yet one in which every blade of grass and every leaf on every tree seems to mean more. Everything is deeper. They discover that the farther they penetrate into the New Narnia, the deeper it becomes. The deeper they go, the more the world opens itself up to them.

This interpretation fits well with other passages that speak of judgement by fire. Malachi speaks of the Lord coming as 'a refiner's fire' who refines his people like 'gold and silver' is refined (Malachi 3:2,3). Paul says that on the Day of Judgement our works 'will be revealed with fire'. If much of what we have done has been found to be worthless, then we will suffer loss, but we ourselves will be saved — 'even though only as one escaping through the flames' (1 Corinthians 3:13–15). Earlier in 2 Peter 3, Peter had spoken on the flood of Noah's day when the earth was 'destroyed' (v.6) and used this as a historical precedent for the final judgement. In that day it was the evil that was destroyed while the earth itself was preserved. The Greek word that is translated 'elements' (stoicheia), that Peter says will melt with heat, can refer to the basic elements of which this universe is composed, but it was also used in first-century Asia Minor to refer to malignant forces that separate humans from God (cf. Galatians 4:3,9 where the same word is used).

Paul speaks of the Christian as already a 'new creation' (2 Corinthians 5:17). As a consequence of our link with the risen Christ through the Spirit, 'The old has gone, the new is here!' This does not mean that I have been replaced with a different 'me', but that I am the same person under reconstruction. My responsibility is to live accordingly. Similarly with the new earth. It is the same earth purified. Reconstruction began with the resurrection. However, 2 Peter 3:10–13 does indicate that it will not be merely a rearranging of the furniture, but a complete rebuilding of the house.

Another support for this interpretation comes from the use of the Greek word for 'new'. There are two words for 'new' in the Greek language. There is neos, which means new in a quantitative sense. If I get a new car, then it has no connection with my old one. Then there is kainos, which is new in a qualitative sense. If I take my old car to the panel beater to get it rebuilt after an accident, then it is the same car, with the same characteristics, but as good as new. When the New Testament speaks of a new earth (2 Peter 3:13; Revelation 21:1) it is kainos that is used. The newness will be in the sense that Jesus' body was new when he rose from the death. It was the same material body and yet transformed and with new characteristics. The new earth will be the perfect environment for our own resurrected bodies. '**Everything**' will be new in this sense (Revelation 21:5).

Another relevant passage with this emphasis is Philippians 3:20,21. '**Our citizenship is in heaven**' because that is where the divine throne is, but '**we eagerly await a Saviour from there**'. When he comes *from* there he '**will transform our lowly bodies so that they will be like his glorious body**'. Note that our bodies are not discarded, replaced or simply improved, but transformed, as his was. Note also that the passage declares that this will be achieved '**by the power that enables him to bring everything under his control**'. That 'everything' will include our natural environment, which will be transformed in a similar manner. As N T Wright says:

> It is the final answer to the Lord's Prayer that God's kingdom would come and his will be done on earth as in heaven. It is what Paul is talking about in Ephesians 1:10, that God's design and promise was to sum up all in things in Christ, things both in heaven and on earth. It is the final fulfilment, in rightly symbolic imagery, of the promise of Genesis 1, that the creation of male and female would together reflect God's image into the world. And it is the final accomplishment of God's great design, to defeat and abolish death forever — which can only mean the rescue of creation from its present plight of decay.

Heaven and earth are made for each other in the same manner as male and female, and their coming together is pictured as a wedding feast (Revelation 19:9; 21:2). And as Wright comments again:

> When they finally come together, that will be cause for rejoicing in the same way that a wedding is: a creational sign that God's project is going forwards; that opposite poles within creation are made for union, not competition; that love not hate has the last word in the universe; that fruitfulness and not sterility is God's will for creation.

It is significant that most of the basic words describing salvation in the New Testament imply a return to an original condition. Redemption implies a return to a state of freedom. Reconciliation implies a return to a state of friendship. Renewal means to make new again. Salvation generally means a return to a state of health or security after sickness or danger. Regeneration points to life after death. All these terms suggest a *restoration* of some good thing that was spoiled. It will be with creation, as with humans. When Peter spoke in the temple courts of the time '**for God to restore everything**' (Acts 3:21), he took the central core of the jubilee hope (restoration) and applied it, not just to the restoration of land to farmers, but to the restoration of the whole of creation through the coming of the Messiah.

This has been a major emphasis of the Church down the ages. Dave Bookless says: 'From the earliest times, right up until the nineteenth century, the majority of Christians believed that God's plans for the earth were more about continuity than discontinuity, more about a hopeful future than destruction.' After surveying four major eschatological schemes — postmillennialism, dispensationalism, historic premillennialism, and amillennialism — Tom Finger, in 'Evangelicals, eschatology, and the environment', concludes:

> All evangelical eschatologies anticipate significant degrees of continuity between our present earth and the future world. To be sure, this contrasts greatly with what seems to be believed in some evangelical churches: that our ultimate destiny is an immaterial spaceless heaven, and that our present earth will be wholly destroyed. Wherever these views may come from, they have no sound foundation in either evangelical theology or Scripture.

We are now living in that age when it can be said that God's kingdom has already come to this earth in the person of Jesus Christ. Though he is reigning as Lord, he has not yet '**put all his enemies under his feet**' (1 Corinthians 15:25). However, the day is coming when it will be proclaimed in heaven that, '**The kingdom of the world has become the kingdom of our Lord and of his Messiah, and he will reign for ever and ever**' (Revelation 11:15). Matthew, Mark, Luke and John, together with Acts, make it clear that the process has already begun.

Leslie Newbigin summarises the missionary significance of the 'already-not-yet' time of the kingdom in compelling words:

> The meaning of the 'overlap of the ages' in which we live, the time between the coming of Christ and His coming again, is that it is the time given for the witness of the apostolic Church to the ends of the earth. The implication of a true eschatological perspective will be missionary obedience, and the eschatology which does not issue in such obedience is a false eschatology.

In other words, our teaching about the future (eschatology) should affect the way we live now. We should seek to live as if we were already there. Our Lord taught us to pray that his will be done on earth now '**as it is in heaven**' (Matthew 6:10). The fact that his will one day will be done on earth, should encourage us to greater effort, rather than leading to complacency. Fulfilling our ministry as carers of God's creation is an essential part of our witness to an unbelieving world. As Sherwood Wirt put it, 'Man is bound in stewardship to take care of this earth until he gets a better one.' And Christopher Wright makes a significant comment when he says, 'It is certainly not the case that Christians involved in creation care have no corresponding care for human needs. On the contrary, it often seems to my observation that Christian tenderness toward the nonhuman creation amplifies itself in concern for human needs.'

N T Wright, in *Simply Christian*, says:

> Look to the coming time when the earth shall be filled with the knowledge of the glory of God as the waters cover the sea; and then live in the present in the light of that promise, sure that it will come fully true because it was already fulfilled when God did for Jesus at Easter what he is going to do for the whole of creation. Gradually we are glimpsing a truth which cannot be overemphasised: that the tasks which await us as Christians, the paths we must walk and the lessons we must learn, are part of the great vocation which reaches us in God's word, the word of the gospel, the word of Jesus and the Spirit. We are called to be *part* of God's new creation, called to be *agents* of that new creation here and now. We are called to *model* and *display* that new creation in symphonies and family life, in restorative justice and poetry, in holiness and service to the poor, in politics and painting.

And I am sure Wright could add, 'in caring for God's creation.'

CHAPTER 14

A tale of two cities

For what follows I am much indebted to an article by Barbara Rossing: 'New Jerusalem: An ecological vision for earth's future' in *Mission Studies*, vol. XVI-1,31.

The Bible could well be described as a tale of two cities, Babylon and Jerusalem. The story of Babylon begins in Genesis 11 with the account of the building of the tower of Babel. Humans, failing to recognise their need of divine assistance, protection and approval, and obsessed with their own ability, seek to build a monument to their own resources. Later, Babylon was the enemy of Israel, responsible for the devastation and exile of the nation and the destruction of Jerusalem and the temple. They were renowned for their arrogance (Isaiah 37:23–25), false worship (Isaiah 47:7–15), disregard for human life, and destruction of the environment. This is graphically pictured in the prophets Isaiah, Jeremiah and Habakkuk. **'The violence you have done to Lebanon will overwhelm you, and your destruction of animals will terrify you. For you have shed human blood; you have destroyed lands and cities and everyone in them'** (Habakkuk 2:17).

In contrast, Jerusalem was chosen by God as the place where his worship would be centred and where the temple would symbolise his presence with his people. Though his people often proved disloyal to their calling, Jerusalem remained, at lest for the faithful, the focus of their devotion and the reminder of all the benefits they had received from the Lord. This emphasis is especially prominent in the Psalms (e.g. Psalms 48, 84, 137).

It is significant that John, in Revelation, chooses Babylon and Jerusalem to represent two opposing worldviews, one in which the God who created the universe has no place, and the other in which he is the central figure whose reign is supreme. In chapter 17 of Revelation John is taken into a wilderness where he is shown Babylon, pictured as a prostitute sitting on a beast with blasphemous names. '**With her the kings of the earth committed adultery, and the inhabitants of the earth were intoxicated with the wine of her adulteries**' (v. 2). '**The woman was dressed in purple and scarlet, and was glittering with gold, precious stones and pearls. She held a golden cup in her hand, filled with abominable things and the filth of her adulteries**' (v. 4). The picture of Babylon as an immoral woman probably has more to do with politics and idolatry than gender. In the prophets of the Old Testament, unfaithfulness to God is often pictured as immorality (e.g. Hosea). Babylon was renowned for its idolatry. Hence, her relationship with the blasphemous beast. Her love of luxury, always at the expense of the poor, is graphically pictured in the following chapter, which describes her final destruction (18:3,11–13). Also mentioned is her disregard for human life, particularly that of the people of God. '**I saw that the woman was drunk with the blood of God's people, the blood of those who bore the testimony to Jesus**' (17:6; cf 18:13,24). Those who adopt the worldview and values of Babylon are likely to find the existence of the people of God the greatest threat to their lifestyle, quite apart from those who are a hindrance to their gaining of wealth.

For our purposes it is important to note that the setting of Babylon is in the wilderness (17:3). The Greek word is *erêmos*, wasteland. The connotation of the term in this context is of a landscape that has been ruined or devastated. This desolate setting anticipates the 'laying waste' (*erêmoô*) of Babylon itself in 17:16 and 18:17,19. This verb is widely used by classical and biblical authors to describe the razing and depopulation of conquered landscapes and cities. Josephus uses it in his description of the Jewish War of AD 66–73 to lament the horror of the destruction of the landscape of Jerusalem and the surrounding countryside by the Roman armies.

The beast associated with the woman had seven heads, which are described as '**seven hills on which the woman sits**' (17:9). This is no doubt an allusion to Rome, the Babylon of the first century. In the unjust economy of Rome **'all who had ships on the sea became rich through her wealth!'** (18:19). Among the items listed in the cargo, which enriched its merchants, are **'every sort of citrus wood, and articles of every kind made of ivory, costly wood, bronze, iron and marble … and human beings sold as slaves'** (18:11–13). Rome's deforestation of conquered lands was notorious. Could it be that John, like Aristides, had watched so many ships unload goods from the forests of conquered nations that he would agree with Aristides' diagnosis:

> So many merchants' ships arrive here, conveying every kind of goods from every people every hour and every day, so that the city is like a factory common to the whole earth. It is possible to see so many cargoes from India and even from Arabia Felix, if you wish, that one imagines that for the future the trees are left bare [*gymna*] for the people there and that they must come here to beg for their own produce.

Another word that is used in the destruction of Babylon that has ecological connotations is *gymnos*, usually translated 'naked'. **'They will bring her to ruin and leave her naked'** (17:16). It can be used of a landscape that has been denuded of its vegetation. Both Josephus and Aristides use it to describe Rome's stripping of forests. It is interesting to compare this with the prophet Nahum's condemnation of Nineveh, the capital of the Assyrian Empire, whose behaviour in this regard was no better than Babylon or Rome: **'You have increased the number of your merchants till they are more than the stars of the sky, but like locusts they strip the land and then fly away'** (Nahum 3:16).

In contrast, Revelation 21 and 22 present us with a New Jerusalem where both humans and the environment flourish. Whereas Babylon is a city of ecological imperialism, violence, unfettered commerce and injustice, the New Jerusalem is a city where all the essentials for a satisfying life are given **'without cost'** (21:6). John's statement that **'there was no longer any sea'** (21:1) may well have reference to the lack of shipping economy, on which Rome depended for her luxury goods, as much as to mythological associations as a location for evil (e.g. Isaiah 27:1; Revelation 13:1). The picture of this Jerusalem is profoundly ecological with its **'river of the water of life'** flowing through it and the tree of life on its banks bearing twelve crops for a year-round supply, the leaves of which bring healing to all people (Revelation 22:1,2). Water is one of the central images of New Jerusalem (21:6; 22:17; cf. 7:17). This water is supplied freely from the throne of God and brings refreshing life to both humans and nature. Here John draws on the picture given in Ezekiel 47:1–12. There is no inequality here as all are priests and will reign with Christ on the earth (Revelation 5:10).

The Bible begins in a garden and ends in a city, as much of its pleasure comes from human relationships, but this is a garden city integrating nature and urban life, where civic and rural values are combined in harmony. And it is God who provides light for the city and who dwells with his people (21:3,22,23).

This vision of Babylon and Jerusalem at the end of the Bible presents in stark contrast the values of this world and those of the kingdom of God. It offers hope for those who struggle to be faithful to their Lord. However, it is not only there to give us hope for the future, but also to offer a challenge for the present. 'Come out of [Babylon], my people, so that you will not share in her sins' (18:4). Each of us must decide for ourselves whether we are going to live by the values of Babylon or those of the New Jerusalem. Whichever decision we make has profound consequences for the future, not only for us personally, but also in other ways we can barely imagine. We are told of the New Jerusalem that the 'glory and honour of the nations [or "peoples"] will be brought into it' (21:26). That seems to me to imply that all the good we are able to achieve in this life will somehow contribute to the blessings of the new earth.

Beth Utto-Galarneau, a seminary intern for the Lutheran School of Theology, tells how she asked her Bible study group in a blighted neighbourhood of East Boston the question, 'What might the new East Boston look like?' while leading a Bible study on Revelation 21 and 22. This is what they said:

> We saw the holy city, the new East Boston, coming down out of heaven from God. ... It has clean streets in which people can walk in safety and with peace any time. There are no drugs, no fire, no fighting; everyone has a place to live. People are planting flowers and trees ... and God is there.

Conclusion

Pioneering ecological theologian, Joseph Sittler, whose eloquence and insight on these matters remain virtually unsurpassed, said in 'Ecological commitment as theological responsibility' that because of the virtual demise of a vigorous doctrine of the creation:

> It is difficult but possible to get men to understand that pollution is biologically disastrous, aesthetically offensive, equally obviously economically self-destructive and socially reductive of the quality of human life. But it is a very difficult job to get even Christians to see that so to deal with the Creation is *Christianly* blasphemous. A proper doctrine of creation and redemption would make it perfectly clear from a Christian point of view the ecological crisis presents us not simply with moral tasks but requires of us a freshly renovated and fundamental theology of the first article whereby the Christian faith defines whence the Creation was formed, and why, and by whom and to what end.

In his book *Gravity and Grace*, he had this to say:

> When we turn the attention of the church to a definition of the Christian relationship with the natural world, we are not stepping away from grave and proper theological ideas; we are stepping right into the middle of them. There is a deeply rooted, genuinely Christian motivation for attention to God's creation, despite the fact that many church people consider ecology to be a secular concern. 'What does environmental preservation have to do with Jesus Christ and his church?' they ask. They could not be more shallow or more wrong.

What I have written I offer in the hope that it will assist in restoring a proper balance to our Christian outlook, our lifestyles and perhaps also our daily priorities.

These days, many are invoking spiritual reasons for caring for our world. Writer Alston Chase assembled the following list of belief systems that have been drawn on by environmentalists: 'Tao, Vedanta, Sufism, Cabalism, Spinozistic Pantheism, Yoga, biofeedback, transcendental meditation, Ghandian pacifism, inimism, panpsychism, alchemy, ritual magic, Buddhist economics, fossil love, planetary zoning, deep ecology, shallow ecology, reinhabitation, ecological primitivism, chicken liberation, stone age economics, Yin Yang and the androgynous universe, the Gaia hypothesis, global futures, Spaceship Earth, rights of rocks, ecological resistance.' It is my belief that we Christians have reasons that are more profound and satisfying as they are based on the truth of the God who really exists, humans as they are intended to be, and the world as it really is.

There are many reasons to work to preserve and nuture the earth, and many of these are common to all people: our own existence depends on it; we owe it to our children; a good earth provides for more joyful living; it is in the best interests of the entire earth community. However, as Christians we have even better reasons: the earth is of value because it is God's creation; he has declared it good and he delights in it; he has appointed us his vice-regents to care for it as well as for one another; the good we can do will have some counterpart in the new earth. And, in view of the resurrection, we have assurance that any good we do will not be in vain (1 Corinthians 15:58). Perhaps the greatest reason for caring for the earth is, simply, gratitude. The earth is God's gift of grace to us and as Steven Bouma-Prediger puts it, 'Grace begets gratitude, and gratitude care.'

Reasons for Christians to care are God-centred. Scott Hoezee says it well: 'Christians must be staunch environmentalists — or staunch creationalists, to use a more biblical term — not because we have our own best interests at heart but because we have God's best interests at heart.' And as he adds, 'we Christians believe that the hands that are upraised to bless forests and toads are now pierced hands.'

It may well be that some who read this book may find all this talk about God will raise unanswered questions, either because their own background has not included such a perspective, or because they may have some belief in God, but as yet have no personal experience of him. I would like to add a word for those searching for answers and willing to take a further step. A relationship with God is real. It makes sense of much that we see around us, and provides a transforming experience that enables us to live satisfying and productive lives, with some certainty as to what the future holds.

Finding such an experience essentially involves two things. First, a willingness to acknowledge that our lives are not all that God intended them to be. We have all fallen short of God's requirements (see Romans 3:23) and most of the world's problems arise from that fact. Second, a willingness to trust Jesus as whom he claimed to be, whom the Bible repeatedly declares him to be and whom the experience of thousands have proved him to be: the Lord of creation and the Saviour of the world.

Two things happen when we surrender our lives to Jesus Christ and accept him as our Lord and Saviour. First, we receive forgiveness and reconciliation with the creator of the universe. Second, he comes to life within us in the Person of the Holy Spirit, to begin a work of transformation from within, to fit us for his service here and for future membership of the new heavens and earth. I will be surprised if one of the results will not be a new appreciation of the world in which we live. The songwriter George Wade Robinson said it well:

> Heav'n above is softer blue,
> Earth around is sweeter green!
> Something lives in every hue
> Christless eyes have never seen;
> Birds with gladder songs o'erflow,
> Flow'rs with deeper beauties shine,
> Since I know, as now I know,
> I am his and he is mine.

You may well find that praying a sincere prayer such as the following will set you on a journey that will be beyond anything you have so far imagined:

> Creator God, I accept the fact that all I have and am, my very existence, I owe to you.
> I acknowledge that together with my fellow humans, I have fallen short of your standards and neglected your commands and your will for me. I am truly sorry.

I accept that your Son Jesus came into this world to save us from
our sins and when he died on the cross he died for me and
rose from the dead to be my living Saviour.

In gratitude I commit my life to him and will endeavour to follow
where he leads me.

I now accept him as my Lord and my Saviour. Come into my life
and make me into the person you want me to be. Help me to
develop the gifts you have given me, and show me how I can
best serve you in caring for your people and your world.

I really mean this.

If you wish to follow this through and grow in your faith, then get a
good modern translation of the Bible and start reading through the
New Testament, praying that God will teach you on a daily basis. The best
secrets of life can be found there. Find a Christian fellowship where you
feel at home, where you can learn from and receive encouragement from
others and where you can make a positive contribution. And may God
bless you on the journey.

Further reading

Wendell Berry, *Sex, Economy, Freedom & Community*, Pantheon, 1993

Dave Bookless, *Planetwise*, Inter-Varsity Press, 2008

Steven Bouma-Prediger, *For the Beauty of the Earth: A Christian vision for creation care*, Baker Academic, 2001

Rob Dunn, *The Wild Life of our Bodies: Predators, parasites, and partners that shape who we are today*, HarperCollins Publishers, 2011

Ken Gnanakan, *Responsible Stewardship of God's Creation*, World Evangelical Alliance — Theological Commission, Theological Book Trust, 2004

James Hansen, *Storms of My Grandchildren: The truth about the coming climate catastrophe and our last chance to save humanity*, Bloomsbury, 2009

Paul Hawken, *Blessed Unrest: How the largest social movement in history is restoring grace, justice and beauty to the world*, Penguin, 2008

Scott Hoezee, *Remember Creation: God's world of wonder and delight*, Eerdmans, 1998

J Richard Middleton, *The Liberating Image: The Imago Dei in Genesis 1*, Brazos, 2005

Sharing God's Planet: A Christian vision for a sustainable future, A report from the Mission and Public Affairs Council, Church House, UK, 2005

Michael S Northcott, *The Environment and Christian Ethics*, Cambridge University Press, 1996

Michael S Northcott, *A Moral Climate: The ethics of global warming*, Orbis, 2007

John C Ryan and Alan Thein Durning, *Stuff: The secret lives of everyday things*, Northwest Environment Watch, Seattle, 1997

Francis A Schaeffer, *Pollution and the Death of Man: The Christian View of Ecology*, Hodder and Stoughton, 1970

Francis A Schaeffer, *Genesis in Space and Time*, Hodder and Stoughton, 1973

John Stott, *Issues Facing Christians Today: A major appraisal of contemporary social and moral questions*, Marshall, Morgan and Scott, 1984

Kim Tam, *The Jubilee Gospel: The Jubilee, Spirit and the Church*, Authentic, 2008

W H Vanstone, *Love's Endeavour, Love's Expense: The response of being to the love of God*, Darton, Longman and Todd, 1977

Brian J Walsh and Sylvia C Keesmaat, *Colossians Remixed: Subverting the empire*, IVP Academic, 2004

Albert M Wolters, *Creation Regained: Biblical basics for a Reformational worldview*, Eerdmans, 1985

Christopher J H Wright, *Old Testament Ethics for the People of God*, Inter-Varsity Press, 2004

Christopher J H Wright, *The Mission of God: Unlocking the Bible's grand narrative*, IVP Academic, 2006

Index

Scripture index

Other titles by Dick Tripp in the series *Exploring Faith Today*

These may all be read at **www.christianity.co.nz**